The Witness Stand

Debbie McNeely

A Christ To The World Publication

THE WITNESS STAND
by Debbie McNeely

Debbie McNeely
P.O. Box 179
Morley, MO 63767

ISBN: 978-0-9828655-2-1

Front & Back Cover Design: Jonathan McNeely
Back Cover Blurb: Rick McNeely
Layout & Formatting: Pastor Glynn Davis
Editing & Proofing: Betty Perkins
Editing & Proofing: Carolyn Davis

A Christ To The World Publication - Morley, MO
Published for **Debbie McNeely** by: Jostens Commercial Publications, 401 Science Park Road, State College, PA 16803
mccoym@uplink.net
Mike McCoy - 570-594-4957
www.jostens.com
Toll-free (888) 897-9693
Fax (717) 674-6583

Printed in the United States of America - Published July 2011

Dedication

To Rick, my wonderful husband.

You're my hero, my knight in shining armor

and you are my inspiration.

Thank you for stretching my limits

and broadening my horizons.

You're the wind

beneath my wings and

I love you very much!

Acknowledgements

Pastors Don and Deborah Russell

Thank you for such a Godly heritage, spiritual guidance, and your example of faith. You have been wonderful loving parents that always believed in me and for that I am truly grateful. I love you both very much!

Pastor Glynn Davis

Many thanks for all the long hours of formatting and preparing this book for the readers. The night you asked me to teach your soul-winning class marked the beginning of a new chapter in my life. Therefore, The Witness Stand was birthed in my spirit. Thank you for the encouragement and for helping to make a dream come true.

Betty Perkins

Thank you for all your hard work in editing this book. I know along this journey there were a few rabbit trails, but somehow you were able to get me back on the main road. Great job!

Carolyn Davis

To a very good friend of over 25 years. Just as you have created the most beautiful blue ribbon quilts, you did some fine needle work on this book. Even when we thought all our seams were straight, you found a few raw edges. Thank you so much for your finishing touch! Love you, girl!

To All My Children, Whom I Love With All My Heart!

Landon and Shaelee

To my precious grandchildren, who bring me so much joy. I love being your Nana and I enjoy spending time with you. Your smiles, hugs, and kisses melt my heart and I am so very proud of both of you!

Bethany

To my beautiful daughter. Of all your gifts and talents, one of my favorite is your gift of humor. Thank you for my daily dose of laughter. Your name means, "God's promise, song of joy." You've given me plenty of joy. You put the fun in funny. I am so proud of you Sissy!

Jonathan

From the time you were a little boy, you could entertain a crowd with your wittiness and I am so proud of the man you've become. God has used your talents and leadership qualities to make a difference in so many lives. Thank you for doing such a GREAT job on the book cover. What I envisioned, you were able to write it down and make it plain. Excellent work!

Adam

To our southern gentleman. I can safely say that you're my favorite son-in-law and I am glad that you're a part of our family. Thank you for always being willing to lend a helping hand and for being a great husband to our daughter and a loving father to our grandchildren.

Rachel

To our newest daughter, whose beauty goes beyond outward appearance. Your discipline and tenacity to finish a task well, has been an inspiration to all of us and we feel very blessed that you have joined our family. Thank you for being such a loyal wife to our son.

Endorsements

Those of you who have been privileged to know Debbie McNeely need no introduction or endorsements. Her amazing gifts, personality, love for life, people, and God, announce themselves. But if you have never met Debbie, or if you have only known her from a distance, then I have the wonderful blessing to make the introductions.

My wife, Carolyn, and I met Debbie in 1985 and have enjoyed our years of friendship with her. She is a multi-talented lady, touchable and huggable. Her trademark hugs lets others know she truly cares about people. Her love for God, family, friends, and even strangers is reflected by everything she does.

"The Witness Stand" is not just another book on winning the lost; which is something we all know we need to be doing. She neither lectures nor condemns us for not being better than we are at soul winning. Instead, with the skill of a seamstress she weaves life's stories, opportunities, and scripture into a beautiful tapestry of love and grace. She never "tells us how to do it" she shows us how! Debbie makes touching hurting people seem natural and easy.

In this book you will get to know the heart of Debbie McNeely. She shares some of the joys and the pains that have touched her family and ministry. You will also meet some amazing people along the way and will rejoice at what the grace of God has done in their lives.

Over the years that Debbie and Rick McNeely have imparted into our lives and the lives of the members of Abundant Life Church, we have watched Debbie develop a powerful ministry. She is truly a people person with a double portion of God's love.

Like Jesus' story of the man in Matthew 25 who was given five talents, Debbie is doing a great job in growing the gifts God has blessed her with. As a singer, musician, evangelist, teacher, missionary, mother, grandmother, and now as an author, she has given us a great book.

Reader Harris, a famous British attorney of last century once made this arresting remark: "When I have a poor case in the courts, I prepare an eloquent speech: when I have a good case, I simply call the witnesses."

As Christians, we have a good case, so may we answer the call to "The Witness Stand."

Pastor Glynn Davis
Abundant Life Church
Garland, Texas, USA

You cannot afford to ignore this book, THE WITNESS STAND. It will arouse you to re-examine your role as a witness for Christ.

We have entertained Debbie in our home and church many times. I have observed Debbie's ministry on the mission field. Whether speaking to a small group or a vast audience, her passion as a witness for Jesus is unwavering. Prominent in Debbie's life agenda is a sensitivity to the next person she meets that may need to know Christ.

Pastor John G. Nordstrom
Murphysboro, Illinois, USA

One of the charges leveled against Jesus Christ by His enemies was that He was a "friend to sinners." I'm ashamed to say that I can't remember having ever been accused of that myself. I don't think I'm alone in today's Christian culture. We seem to have believed the lie advanced by our secular society that says that the Christian faith is a private matter; making it politically incorrect to even mention Jesus in a public forum. But in Debbie McNeely's new book, "The Witness Stand," she masterfully testifies to the critical reality that people are desperate for hope, help, and purpose. Only Jesus Christ can provide it. She reminds us through real life stories and personal experiences that God wants to save, deliver, and heal the brokenness of humanity with His love and grace. He needs a voice, a witness who will take the stand in the trials of life and testify to those in need of God's great love.

I was challenged to speak up and out by Debbie's new book, and you will be too. How can we remain silent, while people who are suffering pass by in desperation while we know the answer. As you read Debbie's book, you'll be ready to "take the stand," tell your story, and change a life.

Dr. Phillip Brassfield
Founder & Director Destiny Ministry
Springdale, Arkansas, USA

For well beyond 15 years, I have observed first-hand the ministry of Debbie McNeely. With purposed heart, her passion as a "witness" has impacted countless numbers. The aisle of the store, the airport terminal, the busy street corner, the restaurant, these are just a few of her platforms of preference. At home or distant continent, her passion for sharing the love and grace of her Savior with the individual or the mass is simply the life Debbie lives.

To know Debbie is to meet "Him." Her ministry now put to pen will inspire and challenge the reader. Anointed is the writer; read, receive, and be blessed.

Pastor George Lee Glass
Grace
DeRidder, Louisiana, USA

THE WITNESS STAND

Table Of Contents

We Are Ambassadors

If God's plan was only to save us, then why didn't He take us on to Glory when we gave our life to Him. After all, we're ready to meet Him now. Is He saying, "Okay, let's just see if you can pass the earthly test." No, it's not an obstacle course to see if we can jump all the hurdles and go through all the barriers, there's something else we were left here to do. There's an assignment upon our lives. We are ambassadors of Christ. An ambassador is a diplomat who is assigned to serve as an official representative of his or her own country. Not only are they on official business, they deal tactfully with others.

We are therefore Christ's ambassadors, as though God were making His appeal through us.

We implore you on Christ's behalf: Be reconciled to God.
                                              -**2 Corinthians 5:20 (NIV)**

We represent Heaven and we are authorized to be His spokesperson. That's right, we are speaking on behalf of the Lord Himself and our mission is to assist in reconciling others back to God. In order to fulfill His purpose for our lives, we must take the witness stand for others. In the course of this book, you will hear my heart and feel the passion to find the lost and present them to their Maker. You will discover many of my adventures and personal encounters. You will also be given handy tools to be an effective witness. I hope you enjoy the journey!

Now, sit back and get comfortable, while I present my case.

Debbie McNeely
Morley, Missouri, USA
June 2011

1

FEAR ON TRIAL

According to most studies, people's number one fear is public speaking. Number two is death. What? Number two is death? You're kidding! Are you sure these numbers are in the right order? I'm afraid so. Interesting enough though, this fear increases when witnesses are placed on the witness stand in front of a judge, jury, and prosecutor. It's uncomfortable to be put on the spot with all eyes looking at you. The unfamiliar surroundings make us feel vulnerable to the attacks of the accuser.

Often times when God summons us to take the witness stand in public, or to approach a stranger, we feel as though we're on trial in a huge courtroom being cross-examined and judged for every word we say. Oh, and let's not forget these infamous words, "Everything you say can and will be held against you." We can sure get anxious can't we?

Jeremiah understood this fear. In Jeremiah the first chapter, God confirmed Jeremiah's calling, purpose, and first assignment. How could we forget the defining moment in our life, when the Lord beckoned us to follow Him. It's the call! God then revealed Jeremiah's calling, which was to be a prophet. Jeremiah had no problem with that, until God gave him his assignment. That's when he said:

"Ah Lord God! Behold, I cannot speak, for I am a child."
-Jeremiah 1:6 (KJV)

What he was saying was, "God I haven't grown into this calling yet."

After he saves us, we discover our unique calling, our daily assignment, and our purpose in life. It's the reason we were born.

On August 18, 2008, the Lord spoke to me very clearly to write this book. I thought it to be unique that the date was 8-18-08. The number 8 always signifies "a new beginning." To be perfectly honest with you, my first response was, "But God, I'm not a writer," as if He didn't already know. Then this scripture came to me.

Looking unto Jesus, the author and finisher of our faith...
-Hebrews 12:2

God is the ultimate authority. He authored the greatest book that was ever released, and it's still the number one best seller in the entire world. He just requires me to listen carefully, so He can write through me. It takes some pressure off of us when we realize that the Lord doesn't call the equipped, He equips the called.

It wasn't until the priests, who bore the Ark of the Covenant, placed their feet into the Jordan River, that the waters rolled back. Sometimes we say, "God, you show me and I'll go." When He is saying, "You go and I'll show you."

Then God affirms Jeremiah, "Do not say, I am a child for you shall go to all to whom I send you, and whatever I command you, you shall speak." God reassured Jeremiah of His presence and protection when He said, "*Do not be afraid of their faces, for I am with you to deliver you, says the Lord.*"   -Jeremiah 1:8

Just like a cold drink of water on a hot summer's day, you could feel Jeremiah's sense of refreshment and relief when he said:
Then the Lord put forth His hand and touched my mouth, and the Lord said to me: "Behold, I have put my words in your mouth."
                                        -Jeremiah 1:9

You see, we can relax too, when we come to realize that it's His words. All He needs from us, is our willingness to obey. I'm also reminded of when Moses first encountered the presence of God through a burning bush. As soon as his attention was on this extraordinary sight, God called to him in the midst of the fire. "Moses, Moses!" Moses said, "Here I am." Then God instructed him to take his shoes off, because it was Holy ground

My husband, Rick, was returning home from one of his missionary trips to Russia. When he arrived back to the United States, a question was posed to him. "Have you been on any farmland, or veered off from the beaten path?" If Rick had said yes, they would have taken his shoes away from him in the airport. Their message had a very clear meaning. In essence they were saying, "We don't want where you've been, to infect where you're going."

That was God's Word to Moses. He didn't even want his shoe leather to come between them. Moses had been walking out intimidation, rejection, and guilt from the past. When the Lord gave Moses his assignment to lead the children of Israel out of Egypt, he said in Exodus the third chapter: "OH MY LORD!" Sound familiar? He proceeded to say, "I'm not an eloquent speaker, neither before, nor since you have spoken to your servant, but I am slow of speech and tongue." Then God crashed his pity party and said, "WHO MADE MAN'S MOUTH?"

You see, Moses' focus was on his weakness instead of God's strength. He was afraid that he would embarrass himself and God. If the Lord ask us to do something, doesn't it stand to reason that He'll be right there to help us fulfill the assignment, by giving us wisdom, courage, strength, and provision. It's time to take a stand against our insecurities.

Let's discuss insecurities. To be insecure means, to be inadequately guarded or protected; unsafe, to lack stability or self-confidence. These emotions must be controlled when they rob us of our joy, hinder our performance, and prevent us from participating in social activities. It's important to note that our emotions are given to us to experience life, not to control our life. The cause of insecurity is low self-esteem which is: the fear of measuring up. It's the way we perceive ourselves. Women tend to struggle with this emotion more than men. Could it be because a woman's number one need is security? I think so. Once again, looking back on the definition of the word insecure, one of the meanings is: inadequately guarded or protected. Therefore, being susceptible to harm and invasion of the enemy.

And the peace of God, which passeth all understanding, shall keep your hearts and minds through Christ Jesus.
                                              -Philippians 4:7 (KJV)

So now we know why Apostle Paul chose the word keep, which is actually a military term. Its meaning is to guard, protect, and to be shielded. God's peace closes the gap, denying the enemy access to attack our mind. Even though, at some point in your life you felt unguarded and unprotected through the weapons of harsh words or abuse, you can experience Heaven's Military Might to protect your mind, as it is stayed upon Him.

Thou wilt keep him in perfect peace, whose mind is stayed on thee:
because he trusteth in thee.   -**Isaiah 26:3 (KJV)**

Pastor Mike Hayes of Dallas, Texas, told us a story about a young man in his church. He was nice looking, well-groomed, and was well educated, but he was not successful at acquiring a job. Mike brought him into his office and asked him to explain step by step what happens when he goes for an interview. The young man proceeded to share his experience. He said, "While I'm waiting with the other applicants, I hear my dad's voice so I get up and walk out before my name is even called." He explained that his father was an A-1 mechanic and had prided himself in his work. When he was five years old, his father asked him to bring him a certain type of wrench. He mistakenly brought him the wrong one. When the young man handed the wrench to his father, he threw it out from under the car and said, "You're so stupid, you'll never amount to anything. So when I try to get a job I can still hear my father's words." At that moment Mike affirmed to him that his father is not like God and God is not like his earthly father. That day He faced his fears, insecurities, and the scars of rejection, and gained new courage to try again. After that, he became a very successful business man. He had to confront his fears before he could experience a real change in his life.

Mike Murdock quotes: "Courage is not the absence of fear, it's taking action in the face of it."

Instead of thinking, WHAT IF? We must learn to say, SO WHAT! Do it! You'll find what you were afraid of, wasn't worth being afraid of after all.

You see, a judge or a juror does not expect the witness to be flawless or to speak perfectly, and neither does God our righteous Judge and loving Father. Just that we, "Tell the whole truth and nothing but the truth."

Therefore I remind you to stir up the gift of God which is in you.....For God has not given us a spirit of fear but of power and of love and of a sound mind. -2 **Timothy 1:6-7**

Paul was urging Timothy to rekindle the fire and the passion within him; to discover his gifts. In return, God empowers us to use them for His glory. Notice that Paul also reminds Timothy that the fear he was experiencing did not come from God, but from the enemy to delay his destiny or even stamp it out.

We've often heard that the acronym for fear is: False-Evidence-Appearing-Real. Think about it, it's not even real, but the adversary tricks our emotions into thinking that it is. I really like this one on faith: Firm-Acceptance-In-Trustworthy-Help. Faith always over comes fear.

My help comes from the Lord, Who made heaven and earth. -**Psalm 121:2**

Knowing where our help, strength, and power comes from may not be a new revelation or a disclosure to us, but I find we still have to remind ourselves of this powerful truth. I heard this line from the movie, "Evan Almighty." *"If we pray for courage, does God give us courage, or does He give us the opportunity to be courageous."*

Throughout my Christian journey, significant opportunities often came to me unexpectedly. So don't let the fear of what if, cause you to miss special moments in your life. Someone once said: "Life is not measured by the number of breaths we take, but by the moments that take our breath away."

Are you ready for an assignment? List three things that keep you from witnessing and reaching out to others and over the next seven days confront each one. The word confront means: to stand face to face in full view. It's time to face down our enemy and conquer our fears. You'll be so glad you did!

There is no fear in love; but perfect love casts out fear, because fear involves torment. But he who fears has not been made perfect in love. **-I John 4:18**

"Do the thing you fear to do and just keep doing it. That is the quickest and surest way ever discovered to conquer fear."

-Dale Carnegie

2

WHY AM I HERE

Have you ever asked yourself these questions? What is my purpose in life? Who am I? Why am I here? If so, then you're not alone. We probably all have at some point.

The Gallup Organization surveyed 198,000 people from different companies who were asked this question: Do you have the opportunity to use your strengths everyday? What they found was, 83% of the people said, that they don't get to do what they do greatly. So this means, that only two out of ten people are doing what they were created to do. Sadly, the rest experience a lack of fulfillment in their lives.

A friend of ours, Doug Rodgers, once told his boy, "Son, find something that you love to do and you'll never have to go to work." In other words, it won't seem like a dread or just another day to you. You'll enjoy going to work and getting paid for what you love to do.

It's an interesting concept.

I had a feeling of exhilaration come over me at the age of twelve. My mother was driving my friend and I home from a camping trip one summer day. They both got tickled at me as I kept repeating these words, "I'm me!" "I'm really me," while gazing into the blue sky. I was discovering my uniqueness, even though I hadn't yet uncovered my purpose. Though I couldn't express myself effectively or put into words what I was experiencing that day, I felt a real sense of destiny upon my life. What is your passion? What are your personal strengths?

Since 1991, Rick and I have had the privilege of leading hundreds of people into different nations on short-term mission trips. Whether they were in medical, construction, business, cooking, or leadership professions, they could all carry a block or hug a child. The purpose is not only to equip and impact the Nationals, but to create a door of opportunity for those making the missionary journey. We believe that it's pertinent to release people in their strengths and talents for the Kingdom of God.

After one of our meetings in Corinth, Mississippi, a lady in her sixties walked up to me. With tears in her eyes, she said, "I would love to go to Mexico with you, but I don't know what I'll do when I get there." She informed us of all her physical limitations. Then with a twinkle in her eye and a smile on her face, she proclaimed with her southern drawl, "I guess I can just hug some of those kids in the orphanage." You see, Roneice struggled to find purpose in her life, and because of an abusive past, it was hard for her to imagine her life bringing value to anyone else. Well, less than one week later she was Mexico mission bound.

I'll never forget the look on her face when we arrived at the Eagle's Nest Orphanage, in Soto La Marina, Mexico. Her youth was being renewed like the eagles, as she began to laugh and play with all the little children. One little boy in particular was drawn to Roneice and was enjoying her undivided attention. His hair looked very unkempt, not because he didn't comb it, but because he had five and six inch scars on his head. You see, his father was an alcoholic, and when he was very intoxicated, he would whip him with the blunt end of a machete. He also had scars on his arms where he tried to block the blows.

We shared his story with Roneice quietly, and she became completely overwhelmed, with so much love and compassion that she picked him up and embraced him. She was fighting back the tears of concern that he would see her cry and not understand. We were not sure what the little boy's response would be, until we looked at his face. He was grinning from ear to ear. I explained to him the best I could in Spanish. "This is your new American grandmother." He willingly accepted and laid his head on her shoulder, hugging her ever so tightly. You could easily discern his sense of security and serenity. Roneice brought something very special on that trip. It was a grandmother's love. She left a part of her heart in Mexico that week, but it caused her to return again and again, bringing her family and gifts with her. Her purpose began to unfold on this missionary progress, and others could easily see the change and feel her passion.

In months to follow, she was given a platform to speak to ladies that had experienced abuse and rejection. Whether in church settings or to women in prison; leading them through the power of forgiveness and renewed self-worth. Something happens when we make ourselves available and give from our hearts. It's truly then, that we discover our purpose.

Less than a year ago, our grandson, Landon and I were lounging on the patio enjoying each other's company. Out of the blue he inquired, "Nana, how do you get rich?" While I began to explain the different ways people become wealthy, without any hesitation he said, "Well, I want to be a missionary, so I can give stuff away." His idea of being rich was not so he could accumulate material goods for himself, he wanted to give to others. I believe that's God's idea also. He not only wants to get things to us, but through us. Not only to bless us, but so we can be a blessing, whether it's with our time or our resources. You see, Landon went on a mission trip with us to Mexico and he had the privilege of giving some of his toys to other children. That's when he experienced the fulfillment of sharing. We don't have to travel across the world to find our purpose. It could be that God desires to use us across the street, at our place of employment, or even at our local supermarket.

Once I heard Max Lucado say, "What are you doing, or what are you involved in, that will live long after you're gone?" Let's think about that statement for just a moment and reflect upon our everyday life. It's so easy to get caught up in our daily routines and expectations of others, that we lose sight of the real goal that is set before us. After I heard Max's quote, I asked God to give me a short line to remember it. I heard Him speak these words into my spirit: "Live out, what will outlive you!"

Do you have a book in you? How about a music or ministry CD? Can you encourage someone today with a kind word or a scripture? Any act of kindness will live long after you're gone.

Do you know that it only takes one moment of inspiration to bring total change to an ordinary life; therefore, bringing purpose and fulfillment.

"Only one life t'will soon be past, only what's done for Christ will last."
                                                    -Author Unknown

A few years ago, some friends of ours, Doug and Lain Rodgers, attended a church in Hot Springs, Arkansas. It was a place of refuge for the poor and needy. Their focus was primarily on children who had been shuffled in the system, or had an unstable environment. The kids came to church with ragged clothes and poor hygiene, smelling of smoke and sometimes urine. Most of them were hungry when they arrived, so the church provided breakfast for them each morning before Sunday School.

One particular Sunday, a little five year old boy named Drew, raised his hand for a prayer request. He said, "Will you pray that my daddy won't get drunk this week, because when he gets drunk, we don't have any money for food, and I get so hungry."

That little boy's testimony ignited such a fire and passion in Doug and Lain, that they determined in their heart, that another child would not go hungry in their city again. They opened a place called, The Master's Table. Every Saturday, they feed and clothe between four and five hundred people of all ages, race, and creed. They love every minute of it. Yes, it's a lot of hard work, but because of their faithfulness, the Lord has sent them many hard workers to help lighten the load. Remember the classic campfire song: "It only takes a spark to get a fire going." Their obedience to the call, released others to join the cause with them. I can hear my Dad's words now: "It's hard when you serve God easy, but it's easy when you serve Him hard."

What would cause Doug and Lain to spend every weekend gathering supplies, cooking over a hot stove, and then cleaning up after hundreds of people? It's their call and God gives grace for the call. There were many times that Lain was physically tired or even had the seasonal flu, but she still showed up at her post, and felt better because of it. In Romans 8:28, the word called means: to summon, appear, invite, send for. The word purpose means:

intent, deliberate plan, or goal.

After we've been arrested by God's grace, we are summoned to His courtroom. Then, we're invited to take the Witness Stand and speak on His behalf. On May 31, 1991, the Lord summoned us to go full-time in ministry, and like every other evangelist, we thought we were supposed to have a motor home. I'll never forget the day that Rick pulled in our drive with a 1971, twenty-four foot long motor home. He thought he got a great deal, at a whopping price of $3,000.00. That's still debatable. It looked like an old Frito-Lay delivery truck with the typical seventies décor.

Apparently, I still had some pride issues that had to be dealt with. I'll never forget the old musty smell when I first walked into our antiquated home on wheels. I looked to the right of me and there was a huge refrigerator that stretched from the ceiling to the floor. I said, "Great!" Until I found out that it didn't work. Only one burner on the golden stove worked. A large T.V. antenna had been welded on the top of the motor home. Of course, it didn't have a television available inside. The muffler had a hole in it, so we could barely hear each other talk. You had to use your outside voice, as our school teachers used to say. Our children, Bethany and Jonathan, loved the idea of traveling in a motor home. To them it was like camping out all the time with mom and dad, and believe me there wasn't much difference.

I remember traveling in the mountains of Northern Arkansas, in the dead of winter. The weather became treacherous, with a fair amount of sleet and snow. All at once, without warning, we lost all our heat source. I got blankets and snuggled up to the children. We huddled up close, under the dash, to absorb some of the heat from the engine. Rick looked rather comical with his parka coat zipped all the way up to his eyes. He's now driving with one hand in his pocket and two fingers on the steering wheel, trying to keep his hand from freezing until he would switch hands. We finally arrived to our destination unscathed. The motor home only got five miles to the gallon. Think about that kind of gas mileage with today's prices. We slept in twin beds and the kids slept above us in bunks. Rick and I could have slept together in a pull-out bed in front, if we wanted a bar to catch us in the middle of our back. If you've ever slept on a hide-a-bed, then you know what I'm referring to. So we opted for togetherness with the whole family; the good ole days.

God did not require us to sell everything that we had, and I believe it was because He knew that we needed a home of refuge; a place to regroup and to refresh. Trust me, it caused us to be very thankful for our home and our bed. He has always been so faithful to meet our every need. We were so humbled and truly honored that the Lord would choose us to carry the gospel, that all the inconveniences just didn't matter, and we chose not to complain. Our assignment to the motor home lasted for two years, then the Lord promoted us to a new car and nice motel rooms. Even though we laugh when we recall some of the memories in the motor home, we would never trade the experiences or the times we had together with our family.

What would cause us to travel from state to state, country to country to fulfill our mission and assignment? When we said yes to His will, we experienced a strong impelling force to strive vigorously toward our goal. It's an inner drive to accomplish all we can, while we can, for God. Let me tell you, it has been the ride of our lives. We are living out our dream.

Should you find yourself in a slump, discouraged, or carrying an excessive load, then ask yourself this question: What cause am I really serving anyway?

Come to Me, all you who labor and are heavy laden, and I will give you rest. Take My yoke upon you and learn from Me, for I am gentle and lowly in heart, and you will find rest for your souls. For My yoke is easy and My burden is light. -**Matthew 11:28-30**

Serving and imparting into others will awaken the passion in our heart, and will bring true rest and fulfillment to our lives. I can honestly say that every time I pour into someone's life, in return, He pours back into mine. We find our greatest joy in serving a cause higher than ourselves, and will discover our purpose and destiny in our willingness to serve.

3

OPERATION RESCUE

Chicago, Illinois, has a population of 7,000,000 people. They have a total of sixty Fire Department ambulances with only two people assigned to each one, so a paramedic's job is physically demanding. One of the requirements is to run at least forty miles each week, no matter what the weather conditions are, or how they're feeling. They experience very little sleep on their 24-hour shifts because crime is very high.

A fireman named Buzz was asked this question, "Why are para-medics so proportionately underpaid compared to the medical pro-fessionals in the hospital, and not really given the social status deserved?" After all, what is done for the patient in the first few minutes after the injury is the most vital. Buzz's response to the question was, "The pay isn't bad, it's enough to make a pretty good living for my family. The reason we spend so much time and dedication to learning the skill, is because the impact that you have on people's lives and the bond that you form with your fellow workers is priceless. It's something that you can't put a dollar amount on. That's why we do it. It's really just like combat, it all comes down to the guy next to you and the fact that together, you were able to achieve a great mission, which is helping others."

When the paramedics arrive, they're readily received because the mission is clear. Someone is hurting and they've been called upon to help. We've been called upon as well, not by the hurting, but by the Great Healer and Restorer of lives. The question for us is, "How do we approach someone who hasn't asked for our help?" You see, matters of the heart and soul are buried deep. So to dig, we must have the right tools. Laughter is the shovel that breaks the ground.

Common Ground

It's amazing how laughter connects us to one another. I have traveled to many nations and I have found this to be true. We may have different languages, interests, or beliefs, but laughter provides common ground and gives us a form of mutual agreement. Research has proven there are health benefits to laughter. A good belly laugh strengthens our immune system, by our cells producing more antibodies. It relieves stress, relaxes our body, lowers blood pressure, reduces hunger, reduces pain, and so much more.

According to Dr. Goodheart, a laughter specialist, when we laugh, it causes us to gulp in large portions of air, which oxygenates our blood. When that air is expelled, it's been clocked at 70 miles an hour, providing the lungs with an excellent workout. Children who are four years old laugh approximately 500 times a day, while we laugh around 15 times a day. Dr. Goodheart is convinced that if we laughed like a child, we'd have the health of a child.

My sister, Charity, is a prime example. Her middle name should have been joy, because she sure spreads it around. She doesn't take life too seriously, and sees the funny side of it. I've always said, "If you've got a good story to tell, share it with Charity, and you'll both end up laughing." She will laugh until tears stream down her face. Charity went through a stressful time in her life, which wreaked havoc on her physical body. Amazingly enough, her humor remained intact. As a result, laughter was the antidote that helped restore her back to health. She is rarely sick and it's because she knows the prevention. Her paradigm is: "You only journey through life once, why not enjoy the ride."

Over all, laughter provides physical and emotional release. That's right, it is contagious! You can catch laughter quicker than you can the common cold or the flu, and then spread it from person to person. Now we know why God's Word says:

A merry heart does good, like medicine, but a broken spirit dries the bones. -**Proverbs 17:22**

Are you ready to take a laugh break? You owe it to yourself and to others. Mark Twain quotes: "The human race has only one really effective weapon, and that is laughter." It's the weapon that breaks down the walls of defense and disarms those who are on guard.

Hannah's Story

Not too long ago, we stopped at a Drug Emporium in Little Rock, Arkansas. They had exceptional deals on perfume, and like most folks, I like a good deal. When I walked up to the fragrance counter, an eighteen year old girl named Hannah, offered me her assistance. She greeted me with a professional smile and a polished business voice. She said, "Can I help you ma'am?" I readily gave her my perfume request and asked her if I could sample the latest colognes. While she was filling my order, I said something to make her laugh, so it didn't take long for her to loosen up from the professional mode to her real self.

After our laughter, the door opened for me to witness to her, but the line began to form behind me. I knew that I only had a small window of opportunity, so I said, "Hannah, before I go, I have a Bible scripture for you." As I began quoting the verse, her eyes filled with tears and her nose began to turn red. I briefly spoke into her life, and wrote the scripture on the back of one of our ministry cards. As I was leaving, I looked back at her and said, "Call me." She nodded her head yes.

After about three weeks, I received a phone call from Hannah. She was at the lowest point in her life and was desperate for a change. I listened for a while, then I began to minister with her. She had many hurts and was struggling with guilt and unforgiveness toward some friends and family members. She openly accepted the Lord into her heart, and willingly went through the process of forgiveness. While she began to celebrate her newfound freedom in Christ, the Holy Spirit filled her with such an overwhelming joy, which once again, flooded her heart with laughter. What a glorious transformation!

....In Thy presence is fullness of joy...   **-Psalm 16:11 (KJV)**

Two weeks later, during my morning devotion, this scripture was in my daily reading.

Deliver those who are drawn toward death, and hold back those stumbling to the slaughter.   **-Proverbs 24:11**

When I read this passage, my heart was stirred with such a compassion for the lost; for those who are at the edge of eternity, hanging by a thread over the pit of hell, aimlessly drawn toward death, through careless choices. I began to pray for God to use me to rescue them before it was too late. About that time, the phone rang, so I gathered my composure, wiped my tears, and answered the call. It was an unfamiliar voice on the other end, and I could tell that she had been crying. She proceeded to say, "You don't know me, but my name is Mary. I found your card in my daughter's purse." Then she paused. "Hannah was killed two nights ago in a car accident. She hit a slick spot on a curve and lost control."

Mary was a hurting mother experiencing a deep loss, and she was looking for answers. Why would she call me? She wanted to find out what my link was to her daughter, and if I had any conversation with her before her death. More than anything she was desperate to know, if she had made peace with God. What do you say to a mother who has just lost her child, which was her only daughter? My parents say: Losing a child is the hardest thing you'll ever go through and the greatest loss you'll ever experience. Somehow the words, "I'm sorry," seemed so vague and commonplace, so I prayed for God to give me wisdom and words of comfort.

Thankfully, the Lord brought the night of Hannah's phone call back to my remembrance. I perceived that Mary was clinging on to every word, as I recalled the last significant moments that I had with her daughter. I heard Mary's sigh of relief and sense of comfort when I expounded on Hannah's conversion, and her eternal decision with God. I told her all that I remembered and I could tell that she wasn't quite ready to end our conversation. This was my sign to give her a scripture and go a little deeper into her life. You may be thinking, "Now is not the time," but what better time? Her heart was already tender and I could discern that she was struggling with hurts, not only in the present, but in the past as well. Somehow I knew that she was ready for a change in her life. Like Hannah, she released hurts and hard feelings from the past, and made a new commitment with the Lord. In that moment, He gave her strength and peace in her time of need. It was a precious time for both of us as we said our goodbyes.

My attention went back to the scripture that God stirred my heart with, before the phone call from Mary. I got out the big book. You know the one, The Strong's Concordance. Maybe that's why they call it Strong's, because it definitely takes two hands and a lap to hold it.

Let's look at Proverbs 24:11 more closely.

To begin with the word DELIVER in the Hebrew means:
      1.) Rescue. To get free from danger or confinement
      2.) To recover. To extend over protection, warmth, to get
          back or regain, to cover again

DRAWN in the Hebrew means:
      1.) To be carried away (to accept)

DEATH means:
      1.) Ruin
      2.) Spiritual destruction, state of mind or literal death

If you say, "Surely we did not know this," Does not He who weighs the hearts consider it? He who keeps your soul, does He not know it? And will He not render to each according to His deeds?

-**Proverbs 24:12**

What does all that mean? I think The Message puts it in terms that we can understand a little better. It reads:

If you say, "Hey, that's none of my business," will that get you off the hook? Someone is watching you closely, you know—Someone not impressed with weak excuses. -**Proverbs 24:12 (MSG)**

Talk about straight talk. When is it considered crossing the line with someone? Or, is His business, our business?

Real heroes are people who go beyond their call of duty to help someone, by putting that person's safety above their own. Especially when we know that their life is in danger. If we say, "It's their life, not mine." It's like knowing that a bridge is out and not posting warning signs. We must warn them of the impending danger.

On May 28, 2002, a bridge collapsed in Oklahoma City, Oklahoma. There were several stories of bravery, including Alton Wilhoit who was one of the fisherman in the bass tournament that day. After a barge collided with a bridge, the fisherman watched helplessly as car after car plummeted into the river. Then Alton shot a flare at a semi-truck which was headed toward the drop-off. It bounced off his windshield, which prompted the truck driver to lock up his breaks. When he got it stopped, his front wheels were hanging over the bridge. He immediately put the truck in reverse and backed up.

Alton's action not only saved the life of the truck driver, but it kept many more from losing their lives. These people were drawn toward death and stumbling to the slaughter without realizing it. One saved life can make a difference in so many more lives. It's not a duty, it's an act of love, God's Love.

I'm reminded of a story Jesus told:

"A certain man went down from Jerusalem to Jericho, and fell among thieves, who stripped him of his clothing, wounded him, and departed, leaving him half dead. Now by chance a certain priest came down that road. And when he saw him, he passed by on the other side. Likewise a Levite, when he arrived at the place, came and looked, and passed by on the other side. But a certain Samaritan, as he journeyed, came where he was. And when he saw him, he had compassion. So he went to him and bandaged his wounds, pouring on oil and wine; and he set him on his own animal, brought him to an inn, and took care of him. On the next day, when he departed, he took out two denarii, gave them to the innkeeper, and said to him, Take care of him; and whatever more you spend, when I come again, I will repay you."   **-Luke 10:30-35**

The poor man was stripped, robbed, and wounded. The Samaritan rescued the man from a tragic death, by cleansing and covering his wounds. After he covered him with the oil, wine, and bandages, he took him to a hotel. He even paid the bill, and informed the innkeeper to put the rest on his tab until he returned.

A hotel is a place that receives anyone, much like the church. It's important that we plug them into a Bible-believing church that will pick up where we left off. A place where they will grow and feel connected.

There are people that you are around every day, that have been stripped of their identity, not knowing their purpose or who they are anymore. They've been robbed of their joy, and spiritually wounded, lying half dead in the dust of their past. They wear their fake smiles, but inside they're crying out for help, in need of a great rescue. Many times they turn to substance abuse, trying to forget their sorrows, simply, because they're tired of feeling the same pain day after day.

What about the passersby, that we tip our hats to, giving them our half-hearted greetings of, " Hello, how are you doing?"

I remember walking into a shoe store a few years ago. There was an elderly man behind the counter minding the store for his daughter. I said, "Hi, how are you?" He caught me off guard when he said, "Oh, I was feeling pretty good, but I got over it." Then he gave me a list of all his ailments and woes. To be honest, I really didn't want to know, but I listened. That's really all he wanted, someone to care. As soon as I got the chance, I steered our conversation in the right direction, by speaking a positive word into his life. It didn't take long for him to start thinking and talking positive as well. When I walked into that store, I was in a hurry, but God slowed me down long enough to encourage a weary soul.

So many times our alarm clocks serve as starter pistols for our daily race to meet deadlines and fulfill crammed schedules; much like the priest who had so many duties to carry out, that he didn't have time to care. How about the Levite, who looked, but didn't want to get involved? We try to ease our conscience by saying, "It's really none of my business." It wasn't the Good Samaritan's business either, but God's love compelled him to get involved with, seemingly, a hopeless situation and a possible waste of time. What kind of value does God place on one person?

There will be more joy in Heaven over one soul who repents.
                                                        -Luke 15:7

That's right, heaven takes time to throw an enormous party, over one solitary soul. Wow! Think about His love, and He desires to love others through us.

And above all things have fervent love for one another, for "love will cover a multitude of sins."   **-1 Peter 4:8**

I will very gladly spend and be spent for your souls...
                                              -2 Corinthians 12:15

"Love is a fruit in season at all times, within reach of everyone."
                                              -Mother Theresa

4

TRIPS TRAPS AND TRIUMPHS

In the summer of 2008, Rick and I were called upon to speak at a marriage seminar. After the dismissal, folks lingered for questions and fellowship. I had the opportunity to spend some individual time with a man and his wife. They expressed a strong desire to do street ministry, feed the hungry, and to simply be a witness for Christ. We talked for a while, then the man looked at me sheepishly and said, "I really want God to use me to reach out to others, but I have a problem with pornography." I certainly wasn't expecting that, but I appreciated his honesty.

My immediate reaction was to glance over at his wife. Just as I expected, she had a look of hurt and embarrassment on her face. Why would he reveal this hidden secret to me? Apparently, he felt sure that I wouldn't judge him or cast stones, but would hear his cry for freedom.

A noose is hidden for him on the ground, and a trap for him in the road. -**Job 18:10**

We can be entrapped by taking one step off the beaten path. The trapper has the noose hidden, just waiting to choke out our marriage and our ministry.

Top Ten Reviews reports that the worldwide pornography market has reached revenues of $97 billion dollars annually. Every second, $3,075.64 is spent. Porn revenue is larger than combined income of all professional football and baseball franchises. U.S. porn exceeds the combined income of ABC, CBS, and NBC, which is $6.2 billion dollars annually.

One man was caught in this vicious cycle and he claims that it ruined his life. He said, "There's really a hangover that goes with this. The next day you're exhausted physically, emotionally drained, and spiritually dead; and life doesn't seem so great." Pornography is compared to crack cocaine in its addictive behavior. He goes on to say, "I don't really want to know how much money I've spent, but it's in the tens of thousands."

Do you know that over 50% of Christian men and 20% of Christian women have also become bait to the porn trap? The sharks of greed and lust are on the prowl, just waiting to sink their teeth into weak prey. We must not allow them to eat away at our lives and tear apart our families, so when you see the shore lined with red caution flags, simply do not enter. It's imperative that we heed the warning!

Be sober, be vigilant; because your adversary the devil walks about like a roaring lion, seeking whom he may devour.

-**1 Peter 5:8**

The word "may" is used to ask permission, so you have to give the adversary permission to devour you. Our answer should be a resounding NO! Resist him!

The Undertow

In the year of 1952, my mother was twelve years old. She was invited to spend the day at Long Beach, California, with her friend Jeanie and her family. They spent hours riding the waves with their inner tubes, laughing, playing, and having the time of their lives. Before they realized it, they had drifted beyond their boundaries and now the tide was rolling in. Mom and Jeanie were near the peer, where many sharks had been sighted, so they decided to swim to shore. About that time, they heard a young man's cry for help, just a few yards away. He was making strenuous efforts to keep his head above the water's surface, and it was evident that he was drowning. My mother wanted to help, so she called to Jeanie, "Here, give that guy my inner tube and I'll swim on to shore." Suddenly, without warning, she was pulled beneath the water's surface by a strong rolling current of an undertow. Seconds turned to minutes, as her lungs expanded to their maximum capacity. Then under her breath, she called on the name of Jesus to save her. Immediately, she landed on shore. She laid lifelessly on the beach from total exhaustion.

When she finally opened her eyes, everyone was staring at her, including the young man whose life was spared from certain death. Then the lifeguard, who thought she had already drowned, reprimanded her. He rebuked, "Young lady, don't you ever give up your life preserver when it is in your possession."

It's just like the man from the marriage seminar. He wanted to keep someone from drowning, and his heart, being in conflict, was communicating this message:

"How can I rescue someone else, when I'm struggling to keep my head above water?"

On an airplane, the first rule is: "Put on your own oxygen mask before you assist anyone else." It's only when we first help ourselves that we can be the most effective in helping others; because we usually tend to our own needs second, or even last on the list. Caring for ourselves is one of the most important needs. Therefore, our care-giving will benefit others more. Before you're able to draw someone out of the jaws of quick sand, you must first have your feet planted firmly on solid ground, so they're not able to pull you into their trap.

Stand fast therefore in the liberty by which Christ has made us free, and do not be entangled again with a yoke of bondage.

-**Galatians 5:1**

Tangled Web

Let's see what King David had to say about it. Remember his affair with Bathsheba?

It happened...when kings go out to battle...that David stayed at Jerusalem. -**2 Samuel 11:1**

Warfare doesn't stop, so neither can our prayer life. When David should have been at the forefront of the battle, he was at home taking it easy, with his armor in the wardrobe. That was not who David was. What's wrong with this picture? Do you remember this famous song? "Saul has slain his thousands and David his ten thousands." David was a full-fledged warrior. Could it be that he had caught a glimpse of her before this particular day? One can only speculate.

Two years ago, we were in Israel and it was during the time when King David's palace was being excavated. They were still digging with much excitement, since the artifacts were original to his day. Our guide showed us the area where David would have peered from his palace down to the roof where Bathsheba was bathing. He said, "What's interesting is that anytime a woman would take a bath on the typical Jewish flat roof, she would always put a shelter of fabric over the bath area for privacy, so houses above would not have a clear view." Evidently there were no curtains around her bath since she was seen by David.

But every man is tempted, when he is drawn away of his own lust, and enticed. Then when lust hath conceived it bringeth forth sin: and sin when it is finished, bringeth forth death.   -**James 1:14-15**

When we continue to read 2 Samuel the 11th and 12th chapters, we find out that after sin was finished it took the lives of two innocent people; Bathsheba's husband, Uriah, and the child that she and David conceived together. What we do, not only affects us, but all those around us. Especially, the ones we love and the ones who love us. This does not mean that every time we mess up, somebody's going to die. It does mean that we must repent and turn away from it, before sin becomes full-grown and takes control of our lives.

In Psalm 51, you can read David's earnest prayer of repentance. That's why he was a man after God's own heart, because when he messed up, he admitted his wrong and repented. I once heard someone say, "Admit it, quit it, and forget it!" Don't blame yourself anymore. In Psalm 19:12-14, David cries out: *Who can understand his errors? Cleanse me from secret faults. Keep back your servant also from presumptuous sins; Let them not have dominion over me. And I shall be innocent of great transgression.*

But when I looked for good, evil came to me; and when I waited for light, then came darkness.   **-Job 30:26**

When you're surfing through the television channels or the internet, looking for good, often times, evil will come to you. Then you find yourself riding the big waves of pornography. The flesh likes the thrill of the wave and looks for the next surge. Before you know it, an undertow envelops you, forcing you to the depths of the sea, until you find yourself drowning in the waters of shame and despair.

...many foolish and harmful lusts which drown men in destruction and perdition.   **-1 Timothy 6:9**

But, you're not without hope. God will save you, if you call out to him. He administers C.P.R., which means: Christ-Provides-Redemption.

Ditched

After Rick graduated from college with a degree in accounting, he was confident that his search for a job in his field would be brief. This just goes to show you, that we're on God's timetable, not our own. During our first year of marriage, he worked with a crew hanging sheetrock. Maybe he worked with these guys just so I could share this story with you.

Since the job sites were primarily out of town, he would have to leave his young bride for a few days at a time, to make ends meet. He was the only Christian in the group, so it was a challenge keeping his mind shielded and his ears filtered from their filthy language and sexual innuendos. Rick knew that this job was temporary, so he chose to make the best out of one of the worst work environments he had ever experienced. He said that he had never worked so hard and got paid so little in all of his life, but he decided to be thankful and continued to let his light shine.

One winter evening, after a long day's work, one of the workers went to a nearby tavern. Word got out, that he was bringing women to the duplex, where the crew was staying. Most of the men were married, however, they anticipated their female visitors. That is, except for Rick. He was praying fervently, "God, please don't allow that man to bring women here. I need this job right now, but if they show up, I'm leaving."

Laughter turned to frustration as the men, with long faces and droopy eyes grew tired of waiting, so they went to bed. The next day, the guy who was taxiing the women to the duplex explained, "Man, you'll never believe what happened! We were almost here, when all of a sudden, for no apparent reason, the car started spinning out of control. We ended up in the ditch! It took them two hours to pull us out."

Unfaithfulness will always spin your life out of control, forcing you to the gutter and the ditch of despair.

Rick began to thank God for "His Divine Intervention," and because he prayed, the Lord preserved him from evil.

The eyes of the Lord are on the righteous, and His ears are open to their cry.   **-Psalm 34:15**

The Lord shall preserve you from all evil; He shall preserve your soul.   **-Psalm 121:7**

Frog's Giant Leap

I've introduced you to Doug and Lain Rodgers. Now let me acquaint you with their son, "Frog." I know you're probably wondering how he got such a name pinned on him. When he was four years old, he had his tonsils and adenoids removed. As he began to wake up in the recovery room, he looked up at Doug, and whispered, "Daddy," with a raspy voice. Lain remarked, "Ah he sounds like Froggy from "Our Gang," (A classic television series, also remembered as, The Little Rascals.) About that time, the nurse walked in and said, "OK, roll over Frog and let me give you your shot." Needless to say, the name stuck.

Frog always had a kind-hearted nature. He was very considerate of others and had many friends. His curious side and sense of adventure, often got him into some unnerving predicaments. He would just about try anything at least once. It's kind of funny, that one of the characteristics of a frog is that its eyes bulge out, so that it can see in all directions, which is synonymous with Frog Rodgers. His eyes were always wide open to see what he could get into next. He absolutely refused to be down in the dumps or outright bored. Life was a party, even if he was the one blowing up all the ballons.

In the summer of 1986, Doug and Lain decided to take their family on a vacation to Hawaii. After a long flight, they were eager to drop their luggage and settle into their beach front condominium. Their condo was on the twelfth floor, so they had an incredible view of the Pacific Ocean, with prospects of breathtaking sunsets. When they walked into the living room, Doug's attention was drawn to the sliding glass doors that led to a small balcony. Right away, he felt the need to forewarn Frog to stay clear of them. He instructed, "Now son, I don't want you to go out of those doors. In fact, I don't even want you to go near them, and if you do, you're getting a whipping!" Frog agreed, but after a while his curiosity got the best of him, so while everyone else was busy putting their things away, he went into the living room, quietly opened the sliding glass doors, and stepped out on to the balcony.

The wind was so strong that it literally blew his hat right off of his head. He looked down to see where it had landed, and there it was, hung on a ledge below. The ledge was actually a concrete lip that protruded out from the wall of the building. Without a second thought, Frog climbed over the balcony, stretching his legs down to the six inch ledge. His hat was at least eight feet away, so he carefully walked foot over foot to retrieve it. Keep in mind, that he was on the outside wall, twelve stories high, strong winds blowing, with no rails or protection to keep him from falling. About that time, Doug and Lain said, "Where's Frog?" Immediately, Doug rushed to the living room, only to find that the sliding glass doors were open. With a dreadful fear, he looked over the balcony, not sure what he would find. Then he caught a glimpse of Frog on a narrow ledge beneath the deck. He gasped, as he saw the potential fate of his twelve year old son. At this point, Frog already had his hat in his hand and was halfway back across the ledge. Instead of Doug scolding him, while his life was still in jeopardy, he calmly instructed, "Son, take me by the hand and I'll pull you up." Frog just thought he was fearless, until his daddy got a hold of him. You know that whipping he promised, well, Doug has always been a man of his word. Frog learned that correction is not rejection and that a father's love is not only demonstrated by what he gives us, but also in what he keeps us from.

What would cause a person to step across their parameters, or confines of marriage. Is it because they simply like the adrenaline rush? Maybe it's because they enjoy living life on the edge, not realizing that at any moment they could lose it all, or even fall to their destruction. Even as Christians, we can be lured to the edge through pornography, fornication, adultery, homosexuality, and many other temptations.

Jesus knows what it feels like to be tempted. Do you remember when the devil took Him to a high pinnacle? His scheme was to convince Him to jump, break His Father's rules, and forfeit the game. Jesus went ahead and made the journey, so we would know how to make ours. Even though He could have tapped into His divine nature, He defeated the devil with the Word of God. He was demonstrating to us the power of the Sword of the Spirit

It's our only offensive weapon against our adversary. That's how we win this battle against temptation! We must pray daily and read His Word, and not just read it, but speak it out loud against our adversary. Remember, the devil can't read your mind, but he listens to what you say. Stay armed and dangerous with your sword ready.

Somehow, this reminds me of the "Andy Griffith Show." His deputy, Barney Fife, was actually an insecure guy, until he put on his uniform and strapped on his pistol. Then he started walking tall, like Matt Dillon and John Wayne. Andy only allowed him to have one bullet at a time for his pocket, but he kept that bullet polished and ready at a minute's notice.

God gives us our ammunition daily for one battle at a time. It's imperative that we stay alert, and one step ahead of the enemy. Now, Barney's aim wasn't always on target. In fact, he nearly shot himself in the foot several times, but Andy never exposed Barney's weaknesses to others, and neither does God expose ours when we miss the mark. As we come before Him, with a heart of repentance, He gives us another chance to try again. When we uncover our sins, He covers us with His amazing love. Remember when Adam and Eve sinned in the garden and discovered their nakedness? They were forced to leave the place where they had messed up, but before they departed, God covered them.

He who covers his sins will not prosper, but whoever confesses and forsakes them will have mercy. **-Proverbs 28:13**

Blessed is he whose transgression is forgiven, whose sin is covered. **-Psalm 32:1**

Once again, He's got us covered!

The reason Frog made such a risky decision is not because he lost his hat, but because he walked away from his Father's presence. You see, it wasn't until he ignored the warning and walked away from the umbrella of protection, that the winds of adversity took something of value from him. At that point, he found himself out on a ledge, completely alone and vulnerable. Even in our pursuit to obtain something we've lost, God comes looking for us. Just like Doug went looking for Frog. In spite of what we've done or how far we've strayed, our Heavenly Father reaches out for us, lifts us up from our predicament, corrects us and loves us like it never happened.

I will seek what was lost and bring back what was driven away,
bind up the broken and strengthen what was sick...

-Ezekiel 34:16

Let's refer back to the couple from the marriage seminar. I took some time to minister with both of them. First of all, I pulled her into the conversation and made him aware of how his actions affected his wife. She experienced hurt, insecurity, distrust, betrayal, resentment, and a feeling of worthlessness. Every time he looked at a porn site, she felt like he was having an affair on her. Maybe that's why Jesus took the seventh commandment to another level.

"You have heard that it was said to those of old, 'You shall not commit adultery.' But I say to you that whoever looks at a woman to lust for her has already committed adultery with her in his heart."

-Matthew 5:27-28

I shared with them the need for praying together and spending time with each other. I conveyed the importance of honest communication and accountability, without any hidden secrets!

Apostle Paul gives us the escape route from allurement and temptation.

Wherefore let him that thinketh he standeth take heed lest he fall.
There hath no temptation taken you but such as is common to man:

but God is faithful, who will not suffer you to be tempted above that ye are able; but will with the temptation also make a way to escape, that ye may be able to bear it. -1 **Corinthians 10:12-13 (KJV)**

We cannot navigate our way through life without God's moral compass. We need Him and each another.

With a deep regret and tears streaming down his face, he said, "Honey, I am so sorry that I have hurt you." He told her that he was coming clean and that he desperately wanted God to reconcile their marriage. I asked them to embrace while I prayed over them. After prayer, she forgave him, and they expressed their love to each other.

I understand that it takes time for trust to be earned and proven, but they are on their way to total recovery, as they continue to grow together in their marriage and their ministry.

Now thanks be to God who always leads us in triumph in Christ...
-2 **Corinthians 2:14**

5

HEALING FOR THE BACKSLIDER

An issue of Eternity Magazine reported the results of an evangelistic crusade that involved 178 churches. Out of 4,106 decisions for Christ, only 3% joined a local church. Another crusade reported 6,000 decisions, but after follow-up and counsel, 947 had already backslidden within the first three months. If an average sinner looked at these disturbing statistics, they would find it to be insurmountable; therefore, they would refuse to make a commitment to God, or even try. Have you ever heard someone say, "I'm not going to serve God, until I know I can do it right and do it all the way?" Their fear of failure keeps them from even stepping up to the plate.

When our son, Jonathan, was twelve years old, he joined Little League. We noticed that he seemed a little hesitant in swinging the bat, for fear that he would strike out. Finally Rick said, "Son, there's no shame in striking out, as long as you're swinging the bat." He went on to say, "Babe Ruth held the record for the most homeruns, but what many people don't remember is, he also held the record for the most strike outs." After that little pep talk, Jonathan began to swing the bat and connect with the ball. Within three weeks, his batting average skyrocketed to seven hundred. Because he decided to try, he was awarded a trophy at the end of the season for the best batting average.

Being afraid to make a move for God, is like someone standing on the deck of a sinking ship and saying, "I'm not going to jump, until I learn how to swim."

When Rick was five years old, his father took their family to Crab Orchard Lake, in Southern Illinois. He was standing on a big rock, when his father told him to jump to him. He knew the water was well over his head, so he was very apprehensive to make the move. Then his father said, "Son, don't you trust me?" After that, he jumped. He went under the water, and for a brief moment he was frightened, but then he felt his father's big hands lift him up. He said, "Kick son, today, you're going to learn how to swim!"

You see, God teaches us how to swim after we jump in, so we need to go ahead and jump. He'll catch us and lift us up again, even when life takes us in over our head.

Now unto Him that is able to keep you from falling, and to present you faultless before the presence of His glory with exceeding joy.

-**Jude 24 (KJV)**

This scripture does not mean perfection, or that we'll be without faults, it means, that He'll guard and preserve us, as long as we just hang on to Him.

Why do people backslide? I believe Matthew the thirteenth chapter describes it best. Jesus paints the picture for them. He told the parable of a farmer who went out to sow some grain. He said there were some seeds that fell on stony ground. The seeds quickly sprouted because there was very little depth, and when the sun came up, the plants burned, dried up, and withered away. He explained, the seeds that fell on stony ground stood for the people who received the message gladly. The seed of His Word didn't sink deep inside of them; therefore, when trouble or offences came they gave up at once.

That's why it's proven, that "One on one" witnessing, is the most effective. It's our job to reach out to them in our everyday life, because before we can connect them to a local church, they need to feel connected to us. It has been said that if a person doesn't make a friend within three weeks of coming to your church, they will eventually leave or get lost in the crowd. They need connectivity, involvement, and fellowship while they're being rooted and grounded in the Word. They may come in feeling like a potted plant that is dependent upon others to water them, but if we take the time, they can become: ...*like a tree planted by the rivers of water, that brings forth its fruit in its season, whose leaf also shall not wither; and whatever he does shall prosper.*   -Psalm 1:3

Frog's Bailout

In the summer of 1974, Doug and Lain decided to take a drive. It was such a beautiful Sunday afternoon, that they opened the sunroof of their car to let in some sunshine and fresh air. After they secured their two small children in the back seat, they proceeded on their journey. Doug had accelerated to thirty miles an hour, when he heard a tapping noise on the rear glass of the car. They both looked behind them, only to see the impending danger of their two year old son.

In the course of Doug and Lain's conversation, Frog had climbed out of the sunroof onto the trunk, and was looking at them through the window with a big smile on his face. He was knocking on the glass with one hand and waving at them with the other. Immediately, their hearts pulsed with fear, so with Lain's maternal instincts, she screamed, "Stop!"

We all know what would have happened if Doug would have come to an abrupt halt, so he gathered his emotions and gradually slowed down. Before Doug came to a complete stop, Frog had already climbed back into the sunroof, finding his position in the back seat. Whoa, that was close!

I can just hear their sigh of relief, along with correction and instruction to their little blonde-haired, blue-eyed boy. How ironic that the acronym for F.R.O.G. is: Fully-Relying-On-God. Trust me, Doug and Lain were doing that before the bracelets and t-shirts were printed.

Marie Eber Von Eschenbach quotes: *"In youth we learn, in age we understand."* (I know, "Her name is almost as long as the quote.")

Often times, it takes a few memorable experiences to finally understand what we've learned. It all begins with, "No no!" "Don't touch that!" "Get down!" "It'll bite you!" "Don't climb on that," and the list goes on and on. At an early age, we learn our boundaries and we're made aware of all the danger zones. Yet as we grow, there's something that drives us to go beyond our limitations, push the envelope, and bend the rules a little. Why is it that every time we see a red button that reads, "Do Not Touch!" we feel the urge to touch it.

Apostle Paul came to the understanding: *I find then a law, that, when I would do good, evil is present with me.* -**Romans 7:21 (KJV)**

This is how it reads in "The Message." *It happens so regularly that it's predictable. The moment I decide to do good, sin is there to trip me up.*

Paul realized, that having confidence in his own goodness and moral excellence, would eventually lead to failure, so he came to this conclusion:

Oh wretched man that I am! Who will deliver me from this body of death? I thank God - through Jesus Christ our Lord!
                                                    -**Romans 7:24-25**

The word "wretched" in this scripture means: unhappy or miserable, which are the feelings we experience when we walk away from God and His people. Paul wasn't a new Christian when he wrote the book of Romans. He was at least twenty years on his journey with God, but he still had to contend with his sin nature; the enemy of the flesh.

Thus I fight: not as one who beats the air. But I discipline my body and bring it into subjection, lest when I have preached to others, I myself should become disqualified. -**1 Corinthians 9:27**

You see, because he didn't give up the fight, Christ entered the ring with him, giving him strength for the battle. Then Paul breaks forth in a triumphant praise to God, for the victory over his flesh, through Jesus Christ our Lord.

My parents raised eight children, so the front seat of the car required seniority. The oldest child would be allowed the privilege to sit up front with mom and dad. Most of the time, the younger kids sat in the very backseat of the station wagon, which was facing the opposite direction. We were only able to see where we had been, instead of where we were going. Webster's Dictionary defines "backseat" as the "inferior position."

Sometimes when the road gets rough, we become backseat drivers, which is the inferior position. Then we question God, our Superior, of His driving methods. He's already been there. He knows the way. In fact, He is the way, but if we haven't had our daily fine tune-up, we'll say something like, "I'm tired of taking a backseat to this situation."

Like Frog, we bail out of the sunroof, our covering and ark of safety. Even though at first, we like the wind of indulgence hitting us in the face. When we walk away from Him, we become vulnerable to the attacks of the enemy. Our adversary wants nothing more than to wreck our lives and crash our dreams. Our loving Father is patient, not willing that any should perish, but that all would come to repentance. So instead of God slamming on the brakes to our destruction, He dispatches the rescue squad from heaven, and prayer warriors on earth. Then He gradually slows us down, reaffirms His love to us, while we turn our focus back to Him.

Brethren, if anyone among you wanders from the truth, and someone turns him back, let him know that he who turns a sinner from the error of his way will save a soul from death and cover a multitude of sins.
                                                                    -James 5:19-20

The Prodigal Son

It was not customary for a Jew to break up his estate too early, but the prodigal's father granted his son's request. This demonstrates how God allows a person to try their own wings, until they realize that they can't fly without Him. After the prodigal son wasted his goods, he encountered famine, lack, and hunger; bringing him to a place of humility and repentance. He had so much regret for his wrongdoing, that he didn't even feel worthy to be called his father's son. Humbled, he swallowed his pride, discarded the opinion of others, and made his way back home.

All along his journey home, he rehearsed his "plea for mercy speech" that he would present to his father, just hoping for a place to stay in the servant's quarters.

So he got up and started back to his father. He was still a long way from home when his father saw him; his heart was filled with pity, and he ran, threw his arms around his son, and kissed him. "Father," the son said, "I have sinned against God and against you. I am no longer fit to be called your son." But the father called to his servants. "Hurry!" He said, "Bring the best robe and put it on him. Put a ring on his finger and shoes on his feet. Then go and get the prize calf and kill it, and let us celebrate with a feast! For this son of mine was dead, but now he is alive; he was lost, but now he has been found." And so the feasting began. -Luke 15:20-24 (GNT)

1.) The robe represented the reclamation of his identity. His father recovered him.

2.) The ring signified a renewed covenant and restored position with his father.

3.) The shoes symbolized his new direction and protection.

The prodigal son felt so undeserving of his father's love that he reminded him of his folly and past mistakes, but his father forgave him even before his arrival. In fact, he didn't even mention his transgressions, instead, he showered his son with gifts; which would depict a fresh start and establish a new beginning.

I have gone astray like a lost sheep; seek Your servant, for I do not forget Your commandments. **-Psalm 119:176**

If it was possible, the prodigal son would tell us that even though he had gone astray, he never forgot the Lord's commandments and neither do we.

If we are completely honest, we tend to have a little less patience with the backslider. It's because we feel like they should know better. While that's true, we must ask this question, "Did they really get to know Him intimately?" Often times, walking away is a result of having an experience with God, but never really building a relationship with Him.

You may have had the opportunity to meet the President of the United States, but there's a vast difference between taking a tour of the White House, and being invited to a private dinner with him and his family. Only then is the bond really formed, when you have fellowship on a regular basis.

Relationship with God is formed by spending time in His presence. After you've come to know His love and peace, there's no more looking back. Then there are those, who once had a relationship with God, but they didn't stay actively involved in their purpose with Him. Therefore, the cares of life entangled them in other things.

It's much like the old adage, "Use it or lose it!" If we don't use what we've been given, we often get discouraged, lose desire, determination, and eventually communion with Him. I believe there comes a time when the backslider feels the longing to be back in their Father's house, but like the prodigal son, they are concerned with how everyone will receive them. The prodigal's father made him feel missed and celebrated, just like we should make them feel, especially, since they were willing to make the long journey back.

Working firmly but patiently with those who refuse to obey. You never know how or when God might sober them up with a change of heart and a turning to the truth, enabling them to escape the devil's trap, where they are caught and held captive, forced to run his errands.   -2 **Timothy 2:25-26 (MSG)**

The Break Down

Last July, I was on my way to a wholesale warehouse. It was one of the hottest days of the year with triple digit temperatures. I was almost at the store when I spotted a lady in her late fifties, walking on the side of the road. I know that it's not wise to pick up hitchhikers, but actually she wasn't hitchhiking. Her car was broken down. Needless to say, I felt an unction to turn around and check on her.

As I pulled up beside her, I asked, "Do you need some help?" Of course, that was an obvious question, especially since she was dripping with sweat and her face was beet red. It was too hot for a dog to be out, let alone a human. She responded, "Oh yes ma'am! If I could get a lift to my trailer, it would be great!" She said, "It's just about a mile down this road." I unlocked the passenger side door so she could get in. She breathed in the cool air and said, "Ah-h-h, thank you so much. My son knows how to fix the car. I think there must be a short in the starter or something."

As soon as we arrived at her trailer, she got out and said, "Can you wait here for just a minute, while I get my son? He can ride back with you to pick up the car." She hurried inside to get him before I could even respond to her question. I thought out loud, "What did I get myself into? Do I go, or should I stay?" The trailer door opened and she came walking out with her son. He looked like he had a hangover from the night before. He wasn't very happy and seemed a little reluctant to make the trip. Thankfully, she opted to come along, before I had to suggest it.

We stayed inside my car while her son worked on the starter. During the wait, I began to witness to her. As I quoted a scripture to her, she started to cry. Then she said, "I've been away from God for a very long time. In fact, I've been addicted to crack cocaine for the last sixteen years. I've just gone through a twelve step program, so I've been clean for the past three months. She expressed, "I didn't think God loved me anymore until today." She shared with me that since she had backslid, her life had been on a downward slope between failed marriages, substance abuse, and financial difficulties.

As I began to pray with her, her son started knocking on the window. He said, "Come on mom, I've got steaks on the grill." She said, "I'm sorry, I have to go now." Because of the interruption, I didn't get to lead her back to God. I somehow felt like my assignment was cut short, so I gave her more scriptures on my card and told her that she could call me.

After we parted ways, I thanked God, because at least a seed was planted into her heart.

That evening she called me. She said, "I really want to read those scriptures you gave me, but I don't have a Bible." It's easy to assume, that most Americans have at least one Bible somewhere in their house, but it's not always the case. I told her that I would bring her one the next day.

She was so excited when I arrived. "Come on in," she requested. As soon as I closed the door, a big burley guy walked in behind me. He looked angry with the world, as he walked into the back room. I found out that he had just returned from a fight next door.

I realized that I was on their turf, but in that instant, a holy boldness came over me. Without any hesitation, I proceeded to pick up where I left off the day before. Just as I began to lead her back to God, her son, who was in his early thirties stood up and said, "Ma'am, I'm ready for a change in my life too." He had never had an experience with God before, since he was not raised to know Him. Even though he was temporarily living with his mother, he had resentment and unforgiveness toward her. The wrong choices that she made had also affected his life growing up. He never knew what it was like to have a father, or a positive male influence in his life, so he obviously had pent up anger.

I asked them to take hands with me as I led them in a prayer of salvation. After they released the hurts, from people in their lives both past and present, they were able to forgive each other; therefore, they experienced true forgiveness from their Heavenly Father. The guilt was gone, and they both felt so much peace. It was a touching moment when they embraced! He was almost like a little boy again as she held him close. He said, "I love you mama." Then she responded, "I love you too, son," along with more apologies.

Before I left, I urged them to get connected to a good spirit-filled church that was just a couple miles from their home. They shared their desire to leave the negative environment they were living in and move to greater things in God.

Our Father God, desires to reclaim, restore, and recover those who have walked away from His presence, and He longs to reach them through our hands of love and mercy.

I will heal their backsliding, I will love them freely...

-Hosea 14:4

Let's welcome them back home!

6

GATHER THE FAMILY HOME

There is no support system like the family. Whether it's a new birth, weddings, graduations, sicknesses, and even death, you can usually always depend on the family to be there.

A friend loves at all times, and a brother is born for adversity.
-Proverbs 17:17

We were born to protect, defend, and fight for the family. I'm reminded of an incident when our kids were little. Bethany was eight years old and Jonathan was six. She was the motherly type and he was the fun loving little brother who occasionally liked to tease.

They were swimming one day, when a boy in his early teens, ducked Jonathan's head under the water. When Bethany saw it, she swam as fast as she could toward Jonathan, clobbered the big boy, and grabbed her little brother. Like typical brothers and sisters they had their scuffles, but don't let anyone else mess with them; or they'd quickly go into protection mode, no matter how big the bully was.

When one of our family members are in trouble, we are not inclined to just stand by and watch. We enter the battle with them, no matter how big the adversary. Now, I'm not speaking of flesh and blood, but spiritual warfare. We don't fight with our fists, but with our knees in prayer. Love causes you to go the extra mile and pray more fervently. You may not always agree with each other, but family ties are the ties that bind us together, and nothing should be able to tear us apart.

"In times of test, family is best." (Burmese Proverb)

While all that is true, some of the most effective soul winners express that converting a relative is their greatest challenge. Holiday gatherings, family reunions, birthday parties, it's all the same. We tend to talk about everything else, except for matters of the heart. We dance around the subject, being careful not to offend, or allow ourselves to be placed in an awkward position with the ones we love and that know us so well. Maybe that's it! Could it be that it's because they do know us so well, including our faults and shortcomings? Especially our siblings. There's a certain amount of familiarity that breeds contempt if we disagree or cross the line. We're quick to share our opinion, whether it's needed or not; therefore, jeopardizing our level of respect for each other. It's interesting how we're able to reserve our personal point of view, when it comes to someone outside of the family.

Do you remember when you were a child and your mother told you to half the candy bar with one of your brothers or sisters? It was of extreme importance that the halves were equal in size. If one half seemed a bit larger, then get out the ruler, stretch out the tape measure. Then mom would hear this annoying phrase, "That's not fair, he got more than me!" I believe that it's still the same concept when we become adults. A family member that is unsaved, wayward, or discontent is still measuring the halves. It's hard for them to accept the fact, that you could have more than them, so they tend to look at your past and examine your present very closely. The truth is, you desire to share your half of the candy with them too. You want them to taste and see that the Lord is good.

It's also important to note, that the "more than me" syndrome, not only affects our biological families, but it crosses over into our friendships, workplace, and church family as well. What is our response when our friends, colleagues, and spiritual brothers and sisters began to prosper spiritually, physically, or materially? Even though they have a bigger house, a nicer car, more money, a better physic, a promotion on the job, or a greater position in the church, we should be happy for them and join their celebration. Yeah right, says our flesh. If we're honest, we feel as though it's not fair. Either God loves them more, or they have more favor upon their lives. We measure favor, but God measures faithfulness.

As we stay faithful to Him, we'll experience uncommon blessings in this present life. He knows us, and He knows how much we can handle at a time. It's much better to be thankful for what we have and choose contentment over resentment, and our season will come.

I'm sure Joseph questioned God's favor when he was sold as a slave, falsely accused, and thrown into prison, but he remained humble and stayed faithful to God while he was waiting for his breakthrough. He spent thirteen years in confinement, but in just one day, he went from the prison to the palace and became the king's right-hand man.

"Before honor is humility."   -**Proverbs 18:12**

Even though Joseph had the royal status of the palace, he never forgot the humble position of slavery and imprisonment. In other words, he didn't forget where he came from. God used him to save a nation and his father's house from a great famine. You see, the favor upon our lives is so much bigger than we are. It's not so we can get more stuff from our Father, it's so he can flow through us to others.

Many years ago, Rick was at a station pumping gas into his car when God began to speak to his heart. He said, "Do you see that nozzle?" Rick said, "Yes Lord." He said, "That's not you. Do you see the pump? That's not you either." Then God directed his attention over to the black fuel hose that everyone disregards and runs over. He said, "That's you." He continued, "Son, you can't pump it up and you can't squeeze it out, but if you stay humble, I'll flow through you." It's not about us, it's all about God and what He can do through us.

Remember, comparison causes us to focus on ourselves and our accomplishments, which results in pride or low self-esteem. Both of which, threatens to devalue our uniqueness and our purpose in Him.

But they, measuring themselves by themselves, and comparing themselves among themselves, are not wise. **-2 Corinthians 10:12**

These are some of the reasons that you feel the wall of resistance when you're evangelizing your own family. Jesus experienced the same resistance and unbelief with His family:

For even His brothers did not believe in Him... **-John 7:5**

Since He was their biological brother, it meant that they had common ground together, so it was hard for them to accept His uncommon message of faith, hope, and love.

A prophet is not without honor, except in his own country and in his own house.   **-Matthew 13:57**

When Jesus returned back to Nazareth, His hometown, He found that the people were still in a state of unbelief. Because of their familiarity with Him, they failed to recognize Him as the true Messiah. Therefore, He did not do many mighty works there. Jesus didn't allow His families' unbelief to discourage Him, but instead, He continued to love them while He was loving the world. We learn later that James, Jesus' brother, became a believer and wrote one of the books of the New Testament.

A faithful member of our church, named Kenneth Wheetley, fathered nine children. He was a kind-hearted man that loved God and his family. I can remember many nights that he would request prayer for his grown children's salvation. Kenneth often found himself troubled, therefore; praying in fear instead of faith. One Sunday night he stood up with resolve in his heart, and determination in his voice. He explained, "I have cried and prayed for my family to be saved, but now this is my prayer. Lord, help me to win someone else's family, and in return, maybe someone else can win mine."

When it comes to family, sometimes it's more of what we do, than what we say. This is also true concerning our spouse.

Wives, likewise, be submissive to your our own husbands, that even

if some do not obey the word, they, without a word, may be won by the conduct of their wives....
-1 Peter 3:1

Our families are observing our behavior and viewing our example. One day they'll come looking for us when they're in a humble state, or in a time of crisis. In that moment, they will be ready and willing to hear what we have to say.

7

OUR GREATEST POSSESSION

Let's talk about the family members that are regarded as the closest ones to our hearts. They are bone of our bone and flesh of our flesh. We share the same D.N.A., which can also stand for: Dearest, Nearest, and Adored. You guessed it! It is our children. The love we experience for them surpasses our understanding, and the three-fold cord of father, mother, and child is not easily broken.

Lo, children are an heritage of the Lord: and the fruit of the womb is his reward.   **-Psalm 127:3 (KJV)**

Of all the things that we've achieved and stored up for ourselves in this life, our greatest possession is our children.

For You formed my inward parts; You covered me in my mother's womb. I will praise You, for I am fearfully and wonderfully made....
-**Psalm 139:13-14**

I believe, that's why mothers with natural affection are so protective over their children. It's because for nine months, God uses our womb to cover them while they're being formed within us. After they're born, we still have the need to cover them; which is to nurture, guard, and protect them from harm and danger.

The Long Fall

In the year of 1962, my parents, Don and Deborah Russell, bought a three bedroom home in Fontana, California. They decided to have it moved to a better location. After relocating, the contractor and laborers worked steady to stabilize their house, run power lines, and prepare all the necessary ground work. Then they dug a cesspool. It was four feet wide and eighteen feet deep. Since it was Friday afternoon, they placed a tattered piece of plywood for a makeshift lid over the mouth of the hole. Their plans were to secure it with a concrete slab that following Monday.

My mother's parents were visiting from San Jose, California, along with her thirteen year old brother, David. While she was busy entertaining them, her children followed her little brother outside. They were all eager to romp around on the fresh dug dirt piles. My parent's youngest child at the time was an eighteen month old girl named Karen. She slipped out of their apartment with the other children, just wanting to tag along. Within minutes, David came running into the house with a look of panic on his face. While breathing hard, he said, "Karen just fell into a big hole!" My mom took off running, like a young deer, from their apartment to their new property. Every step of the way, she prayed for her child's life to be spared. When she approached the entrance of the eighteen foot hole, she heard a wee voice cry, "Mama!" My mother looked down into the deep pit and saw her little girl covered with dirt. When Karen saw her mama, she raised her tiny hands for mama to lift her up from that dark place. Mom said, "Oh baby." All she could do was pray and try to comfort her with encouraging words until the Fire Department arrived.

The firemen commissioned everyone to step back several feet away from the hole, but they had to get stern with my grandfather, who wanted to take charge of the situation. The rescue team kept informing the family of the ground's instability, so that they would stay at a safe distance. They put an extension ladder into the hole and then another one over it, so the ground would not be support-ing the weight of the ladder; therefore, keeping the dirt from cav-ing in on her. After the fireman carefully lifted her to safety, the Rescue Squad transported her to the hospital. God answered my mother's prayer that day. Karen had no broken bones or internal injuries. All she needed was a warm bath and her mommy's loving arms.

Do you remember when your children were toddlers? One day you tried to dress them and they said, "I do it myself." Occasionally, you would allow them to try their independence, and you couldn't help but laugh when they came running to you, with their clothes on inside out and their shoes on backwards. When they finally become of age, they get to experience the freedom to make their own decisions, and they really want us to believe, that they can do it all by themselves. That's why they're often reluctant to come to us when they need advice. With some, it's like a young bull in the pen, and when the gate opens, they're ready to kick and snort without anybody on their back. This is the hardest time for us as parents, to cut the apron strings, for fear that they'll lose their grip on life in their transition to adulthood.

We feel them slipping through our hands, and we know by their choices that they're headed in the wrong direction. They don't recognize it, but their shoes are once again on backwards and they can't tell which is the left or the right way. We would like to post up all the signs that read, "Wrong way," "Slow down," and "Detour just ahead." Then it happens! They find themselves falling into the pit of despair and they're bleeding from a broken heart. We desire so badly to lift them to safety and bandage their wounds, but they seem so far out of reach. Oh sure, we could react like my grandfather did in Karen's circumstance and try to take control of their situation, but we know it would only make matters worse.

As hard as it seems, we must keep our opinions at a safe distance, to prevent more of the earth from caving in on them. Let's examine our child's view from the hole that they've fallen in. They feel like a complete failure. As children, their eyes of guilt revealed that they did something wrong, but our look of disappointment felt worse to them than the spanking. They still experience those feelings when they're older. Your child knows that they've failed to fulfill your expectations and wishes for them, so hopelessness settles in, causing them to feel like, "What's the use?" I've heard my husband say:

"The enemy wants you to believe that the entire war is hinged on one battle, but the war is not won or lost with one battle, you'll live to fight again."

It's hard for your child to believe they will live to fight again when they're lying in the dust. It's easier to wave their white flag of sur- render and retreat to the enemy. You may be asking, "Well then, how can I reach them?"

1.) Pray For Them

We've all heard this saying, "Why worry, when you can pray?" The definition of worry is: to harass with care and anxiety. They say that worrying is like sitting in a rocking chair. You're moving back and forth, but you're not going anywhere. Pacing the floor only wears out your carpet, but prayer can change the things that are beyond our control.

The Power Of Prayer

My younger sister, Kim, found herself in a precarious situation. At the age of eighteen, she traveled to California to spend a couple weeks with some relatives. During her stay, she met a man with a lot of charm. He told her all the things that most women love to hear. He promised her the moon and she believed him. Two weeks turned into one year away from home. She was living a fantasy, until they got married, then her dream world turned into a nightmare. He was tormented by a spirit of jealousy, which caused him to be possessive and very abusive. Kim was even forbidden to leave their apartment complex while he was at work.

Then it happened! At about one o'clock in the morning, they had a horrible fight. He started choking her until her eyes bulged and her face turned blue. She could feel her life slipping away as she struggled to breathe. Then all of a sudden, he jerked his hands off of her neck. He even made this statement, "I don't know what made me let go."

It was the power of prayer! You see, during that same time, over 2000 miles away, our mother woke up from a sound sleep and began to call on the name of Jesus, for her daughter's life. She found out the next day why she felt such a strong urgency to pray.

A few days later, he willingly released her and sent her back home to Missouri, for fear that he would take her life. This time she was home to stay. Kim's first church service back was on Mother's Day. What a Mother's Day gift! Having her home, was worth more than any money, or flowers that mom could have received that day. Kim was very thankful for God's love and her mother's prayers. Soon after, she recommitted her life to God and made a brand new start. She has been remarried for over twenty years and they are the proud parents of seven children.

Not only did prayer go the distance, it brought my sister back home.

But verily God hath heard me; He hath attended to the voice of prayer. **-Psalm 66:19 (KJV)**

Then they cried out to the Lord in their trouble, and He saved them out of their distresses. **-Psalm 107:13**

2.) Spend Time With Them

They want time with us more than they want the things we give them. Some of the most important moments you'll spend with your children is when your teaching them the Word of God. Having God's Word in their hearts, will build them strong enough to face any situation and weather any storm that life could bring. His Word will remain with them, no matter how far they move away from home.

You shall teach them to your children, speaking of them when you sit in your house, when you walk by the way, when you lie down, and when you rise up.   -**Deuteronomy** 11:19

It reminds me of a little inspirational book written by Mac Anderson and Lance Wubbels. It's entitled, "To A Child, Love Is Spelled, T-I-M-E." It's what our children really need from us, no matter how old they get.

Recently, a guy named Nathaniel, who is in his mid-twenties said, "I would love to have a close relationship with my father, but every time we're together, it's all about business." He's just wanting some dad time, but he's felt as though, he's rated somewhere at the bottom of his father's list. It's not that his father doesn't love him, he's just allowed life's responsibilities to take precedent over the things that really matter. Nat said that he and his brother never lacked for things. They had all the latest toys, four wheelers, and cars that money could buy. Every year, he and his brother would submit their names in a drawing in hopes to be chosen to duck hunt on conservation land. Their names were never pulled out of the hat, so his dad bought one hundred and fifty acres of land for his sons. Now, they have their own hunting grounds.

What a very thoughtful gesture, but he never gets the opportunity to hunt with them and form that father son bond. He has to continue to work long hours to pay for it all. Nat has been longing for fellowship with his dad. You know, just to be able to laugh together and talk with each other. He needs his father to listen to him, and then speak words of wisdom into his life. Like most of the human race, our kids are anxious to matter, so we need to take time with them now, and hear what they have to say. They will feel valued, and that they matter to us. A lack of attention can cause our children to act in a negative way, and some will do whatever it takes to get our attention. We're making memories with our children, whether good or bad, so let's do our best to make positive ones. You may feel like you blew it; that you've wasted some valuable time that could have been spent with them, but it's never too late to start over again. Choose not to live in regret, just make up your mind to do something about it. The time we spend with our children, and the words that we speak are significant to them and their future.

In 2009, our son, Jonathan, had to juggle several tasks between ministry, career, college, and his personal life. He tried to keep it all afloat, so he wouldn't drop the ball on any of them. In the midst of trying to find his way, Rick spent some quality time with him. He spoke peace over Jonathan, declaring a word that would ultimately come true. He said, "Son, I've already prayed for you and the Lord has assured me, you will find direction for your life this year, before your next birthday." Jonathan said, "Mom, after dad told me that, all the stress I was experiencing left, and I haven't worried about it since." The time Rick invested in his life made all the difference. They grow, while we're not looking, so let's try not to miss a thing.

"The best thing to spend on your children is your time."   -Louise Hart

3.) Encourage Them

To encourage means: to inspire with courage, spirit, and confidence.

We can encourage our children by telling them they're special, and that they did a good job. We can build their confidence by letting them know what they're doing right, instead of what they're always doing wrong. We need to assure our kids, that they have the ability to do whatever they set their minds to do. They need to feel celebrated, not tolerated.

When our grandson, Landon, was two years old, he and I were sitting on the couch drawing shapes. I would draw one and then I would ask him to identify it. I know he's my grandson, but I was still amazed at his quick learning skills. I drew a circle and said, "Now you draw one. He drew one for the first time, so with excitement I said, "You did it!" We all started clapping and cheering, "Wow! Yay! Alright!" After our response, he started jumping up and down on the couch shouting, "I did it!" "I did it!" "Nana, I did it!" Then he said, "I want to do it again!"

You see, if a person's accomplishments are overlooked, it robs them of their sense of purpose and worth; but if their accomplishments are celebrated, it creates a desire to accomplish more.

I can do all things through Christ who strengthens me.
                                                    -**Philippians 4:13**

We must tell them that they're not alone. God is with them and so are we. Show them your Red Badge of Courage. We, as parents have had our own battles to fight through and we can recall some wounds that have been self-inflicted. They need to know that we're not perfect either, only God is, and He's the one that teaches us how to overcome through His Word. They also need to understand that, "Failure is not the end result, unless we choose to stay on the ground."

Courage is not just showing acts of bravery. It's confronting difficulties and doing what's right; no matter what our emotions are telling us, in spite of our fears. One of the most challenging things that we've had to learn, is to take responsibility for our own actions. When our children did something to hurt or offend one another, we were quick to make them apologize, and most of the time, before they actually felt it in their heart. Why did we immediately instruct them to own up to their mistakes and apologize to their offender? Was it because that's the way our parents did it, and their parents before them? It's because it builds character and instills core values. Apologies demonstrate humility, helps to resolve conflict, and it gives an opportunity to have a fresh start.

We, as parents, must also humble ourselves and apologize when we've shown the wrong spirit to them through harsh words, anger, and frustration. When we are willing to acknowledge our faults and failures, it teaches them to acknowledge theirs. It clears the air, builds relationship, and endears them to us.

We were ministering in Milwaukee, Wisconsin, a few years ago. Our friends, Ken and Barb, owned funeral homes. While we were there, they received a call concerning a young man, who was killed in a horrific car accident. He was eighteen years old. Well, their hairdresser was out of town, so I volunteered. Fixing hair of the deceased was something new to me, but I was willing to help out. As you can imagine, I had a few crazy dreams the night before, but come morning, I was ready to face the challenge. I made it through! I even had to help carry him up a few stairs, so we could put him in the casket. They were just a little short-handed that day.

The most disturbing thing in this whole experience was that the young man and his mother had a bad argument right before his death.

Life is too short to have unresolved issues with each other. Thus the reason for this scripture:

Be ye angry, and sin not: Let not the sun go down upon your wrath.
                                        -**Ephesians 4:26 (KJV)**

Don't even let them leave the house without making things right. "I'm sorry," are two powerful words that demonstrate to our children what true courage is.

Be of good courage, and He shall strengthen your heart, all ye that hope in the Lord.   -**Psalm 31:24 (KJV)**

4.) Believe In Them

They need to know that you still do. It's very important that our children know that we're proud of them and their accomplishments, whether big or small.

In the book of Esther, there's a passage that says, Mordecai brought up Esther. One of the meanings of brought up, is to believe in. He believed that God had a greater plan for her, and that her life would have a lasting impact on others. Can you recall someone who believed in you?

Mrs. Cline

Besides my parents, I had a kindergarten teacher who believed in me. Her name was Mrs. Cline. I can still visualize her curly, white hair and her jolly personality. She loved children and they loved her. When it was possible, she would give us individual time and her undivided attention. One morning during music class, Mrs. Cline heard my voice above the rest of the children. It's probably because since I was two years old, my mother would say, "Sing with all your heart, honey." I guess I figured that singing with all your heart meant to sing as loud as you could, so that's what I did. That afternoon at play time, she motioned for me to come and sit down beside her on the piano bench. Then she asked me to sing a song that I knew from home, so without a second thought, I bellowed out, "He Touched Me." (an old gospel song by Bill Gaither) She listened and then began to accompany me on the piano. I relished every bit of her attention. It was now the month of May, which was graduation time for our kindergarten class. To my surprise, Mrs. Cline asked me to sing a solo at the assembly. Even at five years old, I can remember feeling honored that she chose me, so I wanted to do my very best to make her proud.

Finally the day arrived and the school gymnasium was packed with folks from our little town. When we took our place on the stage, Mrs. Cline nodded her head for me to begin the song. This was my debut, my Carnegie Hall, so I took a deep breath, released the butterflies from my tummy, and stepped forward with my little American flag. As soon as I heard the introduction on the piano, a boldness came over me and I began to sing at the top of my lungs, "The fight is on oh do be careful, just make the best of what you've done," while waving my flag and marching in place. They asked me to sing another song, so I began to sing my stand by, "He Touched Me." A hush fell on the audience as God used an innocent child to relay a message of hope through a song. Mrs. Cline had no idea that the boldness I experienced that night would prepare me for my future and my ministry.

More than the accolades, and more than the applause I received from the crowd, I wanted my teacher, and most of all my parents to be proud of me. The old school of thought was, that if you bragged on your children for an accomplishment, their head would swell, and you would be setting them up for a fall. That is so far from the truth. They need your praise and encouragement. It helps them to rise to their next level in life. Once again, they need to know that you believe in them, because God sure does.

5.) Affirm Your Love To Them

We've heard countless stories of mother's obtaining superhuman strength and record breaking speeds, when their children were put into life threatening situations. For example, lifting up a vehicle when their child was pinned under it. How is this possible? Health Science has discovered that adrenaline is released into the blood stream as the heart races, therefore; oxygen and energy is delivered to the muscles causing extraordinary might.

In 1982, in the city of Lawrenceville, Georgia, Angela Cavallo's son, Tony, was doing some repairs on his Chevrolet Impala. Suddenly, the jack slipped forcing the car to fall on top of him. His life flashed before him as the heavy Impala pinned him to the ground. Angela heard a loud noise outside, so without any hesitation, she ran to his rescue. She lifted the car high enough and held it steady, while two neighbors replaced the jacks and pulled Tony out from beneath the car. That's quite astounding!

How could Tony's mother lift a 3,500 pound automobile? Is it from experiencing extreme fear and stress that this phenomenon occurs? I believe it's from a force much stronger. It's the powerful force of LOVE. Tony had no question of his mother's love, after her selfless demonstration. Should our kids ever have to wonder or question our love? It shouldn't take a crisis for them to be affirmed.

There are so many children that are being raised without affection, or that even hear the words, "I love you." You've heard some adults say, "I knew my parents loved me, I just can't remember hearing them say it." Of course, it didn't keep them from wanting to hear those intimate words of affection. I understand that this phrase has been used loosely and spoken without true meaning. When you are sincere, it connects your heart to the ones you really love. It makes them feel safe, secure, and affirmed. Why do I feel the need to tell my family I love them on a daily basis? Not only does my heart feel an emotional attachment, it's relaying this message, "I want to always stay connected to you." It's an outward expression of an inward feeling that you have for them, and it cries out for a response. When these words are unspoken, it's like having a piano in your house and never hearing it played.

Love is the music that touches the heart, and it longs to be heard over and over again.

As the Father loved Me, I also loved you; abide in My love. -**John 15:9**

Therefore I urge you to reaffirm your love to him.
-**2 Corinthians 2:8**

Until our granddaughter was three years old, she had quite an attachment to her sippy cup. One morning, I filled it with apple juice, put it in the refrigerator, and then left the house for my morning walk. While I was still walking, my daughter and her family came over. As soon as Shaelee walked into the kitchen, she opened the refrigerator door and there it was! It was just what her sleepy eyes were looking for. She noticed that her special cup had already been prepared for her. Immediately, a smile came across her face, then she put her little hands on her hips and said, "My Nana loves me so much, and she's so glad I'm here!"

You see, not only did she hear those words from me every day, but my love was demonstrated, when I met her need. Shaelee felt loved and highly regarded. Remember, love is first an action word, then it becomes a feeling.

A Token Of His Love

Approximately ten years ago, our home church was having a prayer meeting. I went an hour early, so I could have some alone time with God. When I walked into one of the Sunday School classrooms, I noticed that they were teaching about creation. They had the moon, planets, and glow-in-the-dark stars tacked up on the ceiling and the walls. When I turned out the light, the stars continued to glow. They actually helped to set the atmosphere for prayer. The stars shined for around five minutes, then it became total darkness. I felt God's love so strong and His presence so near as I entered into intimate worship with Him. About twenty-five minutes later, while sitting on the floor, with my head on my knees, I said, "Father, tell me that you love me." For some reason, I lifted up my head and opened my eyes, and all the stars were glowing again, but this time they were more brilliant than they were before. Wow! What a token of His love! You may be wondering how the stars could shine again since they have to be activated by light. It's because the "Light of the world," entered the room with me. At that moment, I fell back and began to weep, then I began to laugh with an inexpressible joy, because once again, in His presence is fullness of joy. God reaffirmed His love to me that special night.

Even when our children are grown, they need us to affirm, confirm, and reaffirm our love to them; regardless of their wrong choices. I understand that they don't want our advice at first, they're already aware of their mistakes; but eventually, you'll hear them call for you, and your love will be responded to. God will bring reconciliation and they will feel connected to your heart all over again. Have you told your child today that you love them?

6.) Reach Out To Someone Else's Child

....Refrain your voice from weeping, and your eyes from tears; for your work shall be rewarded, says the Lord, and they shall come back from the land of the enemy. There is hope in your future, says the Lord, that your children shall come back to their own border.
                                                            -Jeremiah 31:16-17

When God says, refrain your voice from weeping, He's referring to worrisome tears. We must believe that God will take good care of what we've committed to Him.

"Your work shall be rewarded," is a key phrase in this scripture.

I understand this to mean, that while I'm waiting for my children to come back to their own border, I need to continue to work for Him, and reach out to another parent's child.

Train up a child in the way he should go, and when he is old he will not depart from it.   **-Proverbs 22:6**

It means that they will return to the morals and values that you instilled in them. That's the border; the boundary line of right from wrong that you formed around them, while they were under your protection.

But thus says the Lord: "Even the captives of the mighty shall be taken away, and the prey of the terrible be delivered; for I will contend with him who contends with you, and I will save your children.
                                                            -Isaiah 49:25

If we remain faithful to God, He will save our children. We're family, and we must refuse to relent or give up on one another.

Rahab, from the book of Joshua, knew what it felt like to be given up on. She was a prostitute so she was considered to be the black sheep of the family; but one day she experienced the hope of salvation.

Destruction was surely coming to the city of Jericho, and because of her kindness to the Israeli spies, they pledged to spare her house.

Her assignment was to gather her family home. I can hear her sigh of hesitation, as she recalled the last words of disappointment and shame from her family members. More than likely, they hadn't spoken to her in years, but her love for them drove her past the dread of their sneers and looks of disgust.

They heard the urgency in her voice and saw the change in her life. She was successful in bringing them all together, and because of her love and determination, her entire family was saved.

We read later, that she became a faithful woman of God. Rahab's name is even found in Jesus' family tree.

The informality of family life is a blessed condition, that allows us to become our best, while looking our worst.
                                                            -Marge Kennedy

Other things may change us, but we start and end with family.
                                                            -Anthony Brandt

Whatever it takes, let's gather the family home!

8

THE WONDER YEARS

The wonder years are when young people wonder who they are, and if they'll be accepted. Sometimes in midst of their wondering, they wander off. Lately, I've been doing a survey of my own. I went to the nearest mall and engaged teenagers in conversation. I asked them what their greatest challenges were. It was not a question they contemplated; it was an easy answer. "Peer pressure." It's easier for them to go along with the crowd than to feel different, alone, and rejected. Their ungoverned appetites of smoking, drinking, drugs, and premarital sex is usually a result of trying to fit in. Even keeping up with the latest styles and trends can be a form of peer pressure. A lot of kids feel like an outcast if their parents aren't able to afford the expensive tennis shoes or jeans, that everyone else is wearing.

Our son-in-law, Adam, said that when he was in high school, he would apply for odd jobs in the summer. He would haul hay, mow lawns, and rake leaves, just so he could buy the high dollar shoes and name brand clothes like the other kids. It was worth all the hard work and sweat, just to be a part of the group. Now, this is not to imply, that wearing designer clothing is wrong. I have purchased some of the best clothes at bargain prices and have received fine apparel as gifts. However, it can become wrong, when we allow it to determine our self-worth or who our friends are. It makes you understand the reason why some schools require uniforms. It's simply because it creates equality among all the students.

Once Adam made it into the "Clique," he discovered that his would-be friends had very few moral values. He learned from their mistakes and started choosing his friends wisely. He began to take a stand for God and walk in his own individuality. After that, he realized that it wasn't his wardrobe that caused him to be well liked and respected, it was his personality and moral convictions.

Without Godly leadership, it's hard for young people to find strength and confidence to stand firm, and walk away from the wrong influences.

Be not deceived: Evil company corrupts good habits.
-**1 Corinthians 15:33**

He who walks with wise men will be wise, but the companion of fools will be destroyed.   -**Proverbs 13:20**

They need to be surrounded with good company and the right influences.

Bullies

Now let's discuss bullies. These are the ones who prey on the weak and on those who are afraid to defend themselves. Most of the time, they target people who are different from everyone else, whether they're overweight, underweight, short, rich, poor, or have physical disabilities. Why don't they pick on someone their own size? It's because the odds are usually against them at home. They either live in an abusive environment, or have been bullied themselves by others. They operate with false courage until someone stands up to them. Remember, those who are hurt, generally hurt others.

Last night, I spoke with a fourteen year old girl named Megan. She has been deeply wounded by her peers. She fell and hit her head when she was a child, and recently was diagnosed with epilepsy. Because of the seizures, she's had to take special classes in school. Unfortunately, some of her classmates have teased and poked fun at her. It's hard enough to endure the physical illness, but feeling rejected by her so-called friends, has been almost more than she could bear. Megan said, "Now I know why young people want to commit suicide." (It's reported that every hour and forty-five minutes a teenager takes their life.) Then she made this statement, "I feel like nobody understands what I'm going through." She knows what it's like to be bullied.

This reminds me of a documentary I saw on the Discovery channel. There was a group of male adolescent elephants from South Africa that formed a gang. They started uprooting trees, tearing up villages, and terrorizing people. These juvenile delinquents would destroy anything in their path. They behaved like rebellious thugs, as they literally stirred up dust everywhere they went. It appeared as though they were trying to get attention and were obviously full of anger. The natives were afraid to venture too far out, for fear of their lives. To their discovery, the elephants were all orphans. Either their mothers were killed by poachers, or they were abandoned. The trauma they experienced was still etched in their memory, so they took their hurt and anger out on whatever or whoever was around.

The Animal Reserve decided to do an experiment. They brought in two full-grown male elephants among the unruly bunch. The bulls can grow to eleven feet tall and weigh as much as 16,000 pounds. So you can imagine how the earth rumbled and the ground shook, as they made their entrance. The first thing they did was raise their trunks, and sound their trumpets for order and attention. The young bullies stood still in their tracks and immediately settled down. Everyone was amazed at how they willingly submitted to their authorities. From that day forward, they followed them and their example, and were no longer a threat to the villagers.

The elephants, like all adolescents, not only need the nurturing and guidance from a mother, they need a fatherly influence for leadership and discipline. Remember, behavior patterns don't come naturally, they're taught by example.

Thankfully, Megan's parents and siblings have given her love and support through this difficult time. She's small for her age and very shy, but she has decided to face her giant and her fears. She has written a report on her condition and is presenting it in front of her school. Medical Specialist on epilepsy are joining her from St. Louis, Missouri, to educate her classmates on the subject. Megan has made a courageous stand to spare other kids from the bullying that she's gone through. God will use her in this endeavor, give her boldness, and allow her to gain the respect of many.

And Saul said to David, "You are not able to go against this Philistine to fight with him; for you are a youth, and he a man of war from his youth."   **-1 Samuel 17:33**

You see, Goliath was raised in a war zone, just like many of the youth today, and like a trained pit bull, he lived to fight. For forty days he bullied the children of Israel, until their hearts failed them with fear. God used a young man named David to face down the giant, who was nine feet and nine inches tall.

And David said to Saul, "Let no man's heart fail because of him; thy servant will go and fight with this Philistine."   **-1 Samuel 17:32**

David knew that Goliath was using tactics of intimidation, so he called his bluff even while the giant jeered him and called him names.

"Then all this assembly shall know that the Lord does not save with sword and spear; for the battle is the Lord's, and He will give you into our hands."   -1 Samuel 17:47

God's not encouraging us to throw rocks at our enemies, for the battle is the Lord's; but He is telling us to stand our ground and not be afraid. David hit Goliath right between the eyes, which was the part that was vulnerable and exposed. Those who browbeat and harass others have had their eyes exposed and their minds unprotected from evil. We can hit them right between the eyes with our courage, a true example, and most of all, the love of God which is what they really need. There's a reason why Jesus said:

"Love your enemies, bless them that curse you, do good to them that hate you, and pray for them which spitefully use you and persecute you."   -Matthew 5:44

It's because love wins over and conquers all!

A pastor friend of ours told us about a bitter old man named Tom. He was a thorn in his side. He ridiculed the pastor, the church, and his precious wife, Polly, for attending there. One day, Pastor Earl, came across Romans 12:21 during his morning devotion. It reads: *Do not be overcome by evil, but overcome evil with good.*

Right away, Polly's husband came to his mind, so he decided to kill him with kindness. Everyday, for the next month, he would drive five miles out of his way to pass in front of this man's house. Nine times out of ten, Tom would be in his front yard, so the pastor would honk his horn and give him a jolly wave. The man would turn his head and walk inside. One night, he asked his wife to bake Tom a pie. The next day he took it to his house. This time the man was not outside, so he walked up to the front door. Surprisingly, Tom opened the door. Pastor Earl said, "My wife baked you this pie, I thought you'd enjoy it." The man jerked it out of his hand and closed the door in his face. He thought, "Well, that went over good."

Then one Sunday morning, while the pastor was ministering, the front door of the church opened. It was Tom. He crossed the threshold, nearly ran down the aisle, and fell on his knees at the altar. Then he looked up at the pastor and said, "Preacher, I tried to hate you, but you just wouldn't let me."

Tom's salvation wasn't a result of being invited to church, it was because Pastor Earl was willing to go the extra mile to illustrate the love of God. As a result, love overpowered hate.

Meagan, David, and Pastor Earl are prime examples that it only takes the courage of one, to bridge the gap, so others can get across safe and sound.

Looking For Love

Let's talk about our young girls. They feel as though they're in a daily competition for the prettiest, smartest, and most popular contest at school; and so many feel like losers. They measure themselves by the weekly tabloids of supermodels and Hollywood actors, who are made to look flawless by makeup artists and air-brushed photography. It's sad to say, but countless teenagers express the lack of communication they receive at home. They desire to talk to their parents, but they feel disconnected and afraid that they'll be misunderstood. They long for their mothers to teach them the absolutes and their fathers to declare their worth and beauty. Sometimes a young girl's desire for attention and acceptance is so strong, that she ends up compromising her integrity and self-respect. She finds herself dressing in a provocative manner, just to get the boys to notice her. Obviously, guys see it as an open invitation to play the game and she ends up losing her dignity and reputation.

Looking for love in all the wrong places, she discovers that she was only a tool for a guy's self-gratification. Now that she's lost her virginity, it's easy for her to give in over and over again. She knows it's immoral, but at least someone wants her; even if it's just for a moment. Then the inevitable happens, the test results are positive and she's pregnant! Recent statistics show that over 600,000 births in the United States are to unwed teens.

Our daughter, Bethany, is a certified Breastfeeding Counselor and

Educator. She said there have been pregnant girls as young as twelve years old in her class. Most were quiet, scared, and could barely read the literature that was handed to them. Teaching abstinence and purity to our youth is imperative. It should begin at home and then reinstated in the classroom. They seem to be getting a mixed message at school concerning sex education, so they try to ease their conscience by saying, "Well, everyone else is doing it." So many have not been enlightened about the sacred gift that's intended to be exchanged on their wedding night.

There's a young lady we know, named Rachel, who experienced turmoil throughout her teenage years. The effects of alcohol continually threatened to sabotage her household. On many different occasions, she would come to our home in tears, in need of a refuge from the storm. I would take her in my arms, like I would my own daughter, and pray with her until her peace returned. She finally made up her mind. Instead of falling victim to the same vices that held her family and fellow students captive, she learned what not to do, and refused to allow others to control her emotions and jeopardize her peace of mind.

Rachel gave her life to God, and then looked for positive examples to follow. He gave her the strength to say no to drugs, alcohol and sex. As a matter of fact, she's in her early twenties and is still a virgin. She's determined to save herself for the man God has designed for her. Rachel's heart's desire is to be a peacemaker, empower young people, and rebuild their self-esteem. She guards her peace, because she knows what it's like to live without it.

Depart from evil and do good; seek peace and pursue it.

-Psalm 34:14

On the flip side of Rachel's story, a teenage girl called me last month and was desperate for some Godly counsel. She became a mother at the age of sixteen, and even though she loves her child, she's felt used and deserted. While there are young men who take responsibility for their mistakes, others get afraid and abandon ship. She desires to be married so badly, that she's become vulnerable and available to whoever gives her attention; because that's really what she's starving for.

She's felt like such a failure and was ready to give up on life. She felt like her parents could do a much better job raising her child. I tried to convince her that if she was willing to throw her life away, why not give it away to the Lord. I began to assure her of God's love and forgiveness, if she asked Him from her heart. I told her that even though she had lost her virginity, she could regain her purity and self-respect. It was hard for her to imagine that God could love her again, because of all the mistakes she had made.

I'm reminded of the "woman at the well" in John 4:7-29. She had five failed marriages and was presently living with a man. The Samaritan woman would walk alone to the well, so she wouldn't have to endure the gossip of the other women. Jesus knew all about her and still loved her. He also knew that she was tired of carrying the heavy load of guilt and shame. When He said, "Go and get your husband," in a sense, He was saying, "I'm willing to give you a brand new start." After He revealed His identity to her, she left her water pot, ran into the city, and told them all about her encounter with Jesus. For the first time in a long time, she was able to face people without any remorse or disgrace. Revival broke out in Samaria after they all came out to meet Him.

Jesus turned her mess, into the message, that would transform hundreds of lives. There are thousands of people that feel like they've gone too far; and so many people that feel like they've messed up too badly for God to love them.

Songwriters Phillips, Craig, and Dean coined a phrase in one of their songs that says it best: "He'll do whatever it takes, His grace reaches lower than your worst mistakes, and His love will run farther than you can run away, He'll do whatever it takes."

But God who is rich in mercy, because of His great love with which He loved us, even when we were dead in trespasses, made us alive together with Christ. -**Ephesians 2:4**

Identity Crisis

Another one of the giants that youth face is "the identity crisis." Understand that if you're not secure in your identity, then you'll allow others to identify you.

I've been ministering with a young lady named Amy, who was recently delivered from a lesbian lifestyle. Even though she has remained faithful, she hasn't felt connected to her church youth group. She gets vibes that some of them feel awkward around her because of where she came from; so she tends to back away and distance herself. Recently, she was approached by an individual who had invited her to a gay rally in Florida. At first she was offended by it, but then she was tempted to contact her. Why? In spite of the fact that her former lifestyle nearly destroyed her, at least she felt embraced, and like she belonged to something. As she continued to isolate herself, the same attacks of anxiety, depression, and confusion wreaked havoc on her mind.

I began to express the importance of an absolute surrender to God so she could experience true relationship, and have the power to resist the enemy. I told her that God desired to be her Heavenly Father. She texted me and said, "I've been thinking about what you said concerning God being my Heavenly Father. That really bothers me. I have so many issues with my dad, that I don't want to see God that way. I spent a lot of years without one, so what will it hurt to spend the rest of my life without one?" Amy said that when she was a child, her dad told her she was fat and stupid, consequently, that's how she began to view herself. She felt like she could never measure up or meet his approval, so she gave someone else the power to identify her.

After much prayer, her heart was humbled and her peace returned. I encouraged her to confront her dad and make the decision to forgive him. You see, we will never change what we're afraid to confront.

She found out that he was coming in to town, so she set up a time to meet with him that evening. Amy walked up to him in a parking lot, swallowed hard, and said, "Dad, I'm sorry if I've ever disappointed you in anyway, and I forgive you for hurting me and for calling me fat and stupid." At first he didn't remember saying those negative words, but then he looked down and said, "My dad was an alcoholic. He was very abusive and he would say those same words to me." He shared his regrets and told her how sorry he was for all the pain he had caused. Then he told Amy how proud he was of her. They both said, "I love you," and have determined to build a new relationship together. Amy called me right after her meeting with her dad. She said, "Well, I did it!" Her spirit exhibited confidence, joy, and relief as she declared her freedom. The decision to forgive broke the generational curse that had her bound. Remember, the only power in the curse is the power you give it.

Amy has made a commitment to a church that is loving, compassionate, and active in the community. She's becoming involved; feeling connected and loving it! Amy's getting to know herself, her earthly father, and most importantly, her Heavenly Father. This doesn't mean that everything suddenly becomes perfect. She realizes the importance of daily devotion, and she's discovering that being alone with God keeps her from feeling alone.

It's important that youth become a part of a progressive Christian group. If you see a person of any age that seems withdrawn or alone, embrace them and make them feel included in God's family. Did you know that most kids responsible for school shootings have testified to the fact that they had felt isolated, dejected, and bullied; therefore, they have violent fantasies and thoughts of retaliation.

A man who isolates himself, seeks his own desire; he rages against all wise judgment.   -**Proverbs 18:1**

We could be instrumental in preserving someone's life. Many kids admit their addictions; including tattoos and piercings. Some say, they're obsessed, and it's all they think about.   As soon as they get their paycheck, they're tempted to get another piercing or tattoo. One young man said that he went into the parlor to get his last tattoo, but before he walked out of the door, he had another one picked out. What it boils down to, is they're trying to express on the outside, what their feeling on the inside. Some feel the peer pressure to conform. Some think it's cool, but others are crying out, "Look at me!" "Give me some attention!" Especially since they lacked attention growing up. They're trying to fill a void in their life, and nothing seems to be working.

What is our first response when we see a young person with multiple piercings and their bodies covered with tattoos? Do we look at them in distain and disgust, and judge them at a distance? God has called us to be His witnesses, not His lawyers and judges. He doesn't want us to try their case, form our opinion, and cast judgment. He wants us to reach out to them in love.

Last year, a tall, thin, nineteen year old boy named Blake was convinced by his grandmother to come to church. I didn't recognize him, but his mother brought him to some of our revival meetings when he was a little boy. He had several piercings, and was all dressed in black. Black is considered a power color that's flattering and classy, but to him, it signified darkness and depression; which was how he felt inside. You see, he always struggled with who he was, because he didn't know who his father was.

He had a longing deep inside to have a role model and a dad to emulate, so he discovered a sense of comfort in food, which led to childhood obesity. Sadness, boredom, loneliness, and betrayal would always seem to trigger the binges. He felt different from the rest of the kids, so he became withdrawn and reclusive. It didn't take long for drugs and alcohol to lure him into a life of false courage, self destruction, and even jail time. No wonder his grandmother felt such an urgency to get him to church. Blake was at the lowest point of his life.

After the service was over, I walked up to him and thanked him for coming. He looked surprised that I even cared. As I began talking with him, I noticed many scars on his arms where he had repeatedly cut himself. He was what kids call a "Cutter." When young people cut themselves, they're trying to release anxiety, sadness, anger, or depression.

One girl said, "When I have physical pain on the outside, it gets my mind off the emotional pain on the inside." She said, "I'd rather my body hurt than my soul." In their way of thinking, it's like popping a blood blister to ease the pressure and alleviate the pain. Many admit that they cut themselves so someone will notice. While others, don't know why they do it. They just know they're hurting, and they're trying to fix a pain that only Christ can heal.

My heart went out to Blake, so I gave him a scripture and began to speak into his life. I watched that tough exterior began to crumble, as the mask peeled off to reveal the hurting little boy inside. Tears began to stream down his face and mine, while he released all his pain. He humbled himself and surrendered his heart to the Lord, and for the first time he experienced freedom, peace, and love in his heart. He gave me a big hug and said, "I am free!"

Two weeks later, I got a phone call from Blake's grandmother, and she was crying. She said, "I just wanted to let you know that Blake was just killed in a car accident." How could this be? He just made a clean start, and had his whole life ahead of him. It was very sad news, but then I realized something. The search for his earthly father is over and he's finally met his Heavenly Father face to face.

He's the one who made him and will give him all the love and attention he's always longed for. Let's take the time to reach them, before their time is over.

A New Sound

You must know, that in the midst of the fight, God is raising up thousands of young warriors with a new sound who are not afraid to stand up for what they believe in. They're not interested in all the religious fluff, they're crying out for a real relationship with God. They're tired of camouflaging themselves and hiding in fox holes, waiting for the next bomb to blow. They're marching to the front lines of the battlefield to do damage to the enemy's camp. Their praise and worship ambushes the adversary, as they stand at attention on their knees. These youth are denouncing their old life styles, reclaiming their purity, and raising the standard of right and wrong; and they are winning! They have finally discovered peace in time of war, and they're not compromising their faith any longer.

All through the Bible, God called the youth for great assignments. You know, people like Joshua, David, Joseph, Jeremiah, Esther, Josiah, Mary, Samuel and many more.

It's because youth are vibrant, flexible, ready for action, and eager to respond to instructions. It's time that we take them under our wing, speak into their lives, and challenge them to great things. They need to hear the voice of a father, feel the love of a mother, and kinship of brothers and sisters in the Lord. We must embrace their generation and give them the opportunity to use their gifts in the body of Christ. Who knows, you may be witnessing to the next Joseph or Esther that will accept their calling and impact the world.

9

THE GOLDEN YEARS

They say that the "Golden Years" begin when you retire and draw Social Security. It's the time of travel, cruises, motor homes, and summer homes. It's the time of life when you can just kick back; relax and enjoy what you've worked so hard to achieve. Rick heard an older man say, "If these are the 'Golden Years,' then I must of gotten ahold of some fool's gold." He jokingly said, "People see my wife and I walk hand in hand and they think we're still in love, when all along, we're just trying to prop each other up." He went on to say, "Yep, you know you're getting old, when you go on a trip and you're more concerned about packing your medicine than you are your clothes." His philosophy was, "If you look for humor, you're sure to find it in every stage of life."

I've heard my husband say, "I may age, but I refuse to grow old."

What he's referring to is; he may age physically and his hair may turn grey, but he's determined not to get set in his ways, or adopt an old way of thinking. He said he plans to be like Caleb in the Bible, who refused to let his age keep him from gaining new territory.

Even at eighty-five Caleb was willing, ready, and able to take the mountain and subdue the enemy. Just because you're older, doesn't mean that you're not able to conquer anymore. Science has proven that as we stay active physically and mentally, our mind rejuvenates, which is the control panel of our entire body; therefore, we're able to live longer and healthier lives.

San Francisco, California, hosts the "Summer National Senior Games" for athletes age 50 and older. Their slogan is, "Never too old for gold."

Charles Modlin started his track career in 1989 when he was 64. His wife would drive him to a town nine miles away, and then he would run all the way back home. He is now 84 years old and is still America's fastest man for his age.

Have you ever heard of Anna Mary Robertson Moses, better known as "Grandma Moses?" She began her career of painting in her late seventies. Encyclopedia Britannica states that she produced about 2,000 paintings in her lifetime. On her 100th birthday in 1960, New York Governor, Nelson Rockefeller, proclaimed a "Grandma Moses Day" in her honor. She lived to be 101 years old, and in the last year of her life, she painted twenty-five pictures. As a matter of fact, one of her paintings sold for 1.2 million dollars, after her death. Her inspiring accomplishments were passed on to others, after she passed on to meet her Maker. Grandma Moses was known for this quote: "Life is what you make it, always has been, always will be."

In the course of writing this chapter, a classy lady walked up to me after one of our meetings. She was called upon to lead the choir, but because of her age, she's felt inadequate. Melrie just turned seventy. Now this is not a woman who is set in her ways; she has grown with the times in her style and music. She has a great voice and a powerful anointing, but age has caused her to question her ability and calling. Right away, I reminded her of this scripture:

Those who are planted in the house of the Lord shall flourish in the courts of our God. They shall still bear fruit in old age; they shall be fresh and flourishing, to declare that the Lord is upright...........
                                                    -Psalm 92:13-15

It's only when we refuse to go to the next level, that we stop increasing in our gifts and ministry. As long as we continue to pour out of ourselves, we'll continue to flourish, and have an abundant supply. Remember the widow in 2 Kings the fourth chapter? She cried to the prophet because creditors were going to take her sons away. Elisha asked the widow what she had in her house. Her response was, "I don't have anything in my house, except a little pot of oil." Just as our hearts serve as the dwelling place for the Lord, we sometimes feel empty and that we have nothing left in our house to give.

Elisha was getting ready to teach her God's principle of multiplication. He said, "Go and borrow all the vessels you can find from your neighbors." Then, he told her to shut the door behind her and pour her last bit of oil into the borrowed vessels. Miraculously, the oil multiplied and continued to flow, until there were no more empty vessels to pour into. It's when we shut the door to our doubts and fears, use what we have, and pour into others, that God brings the increase. As we pour out, He pours back in and fills us up again.

Noah worked more than one hundred years on the greatest assignment of his life. After the mission was accomplished, he hung up his tools, planted a vineyard, and got drunk. Why? Because he felt like nobody needed an ark anymore. Think about it! He lived three hundred and fifty years after the flood. There were still more generations that needed to hear of God's saving power and protection through the storm. We cannot camp out in yesterday's victory, there's still new ground to cover today.

Even the Bible talks about grey hair being a crown of glory. It's a symbol of beauty, wisdom, and experience. While this is true, so many of the elderly feel like their beauty has long faded with time and no one really wants to hear about their experiences. They feel like such a burden when they have to depend on others to care for them or take them places. They simply feel worthless, unless they discover that their purpose doesn't end when their body ages.

The Broken Shovel

From 1958 to 1962, my parents served as missionaries to the Navajo Indians in Continental Divide, New Mexico. They sold everything they had and joined my grandparents on the mission field. Even though they were uncertain of where their journey would lead them, they were eager to follow God's will. This was not a vacation or a stroll through the park; it was hard physical labor, not to mention their primitive living conditions. Oh sure, they had their share of blisters and occasional aches and pains, but the Lord always gave them the resilience they needed to face each new day. They were contented and fulfilled. It reminds me of this scripture:

For You, Lord, have made me glad through Your work; I will triumph in the works of Your hands. -**Psalm 92:4**

Many of the Indians were hungry for God, while others were just hungry for their generosity. They gave them food and clothing and served a hot meal each Sunday after church, well, except for one Sunday. When there wasn't a meal prepared, a big man spoke up and said, "No more food, no more Jesus!" He felt like he had done them a favor by listening to the sermon, so now it was time for his end of the deal. Obviously, there was a real need for salvation and discipleship.

On one particular day, a sixteen year old girl came to the mission for food and clothing. Her ride left, so she asked my father and mother to take her home. They were very busy with other responsibilities, but they agreed since it was only a half hour away. The rough trip through the mountains seemed every bit of two hours, instead of thirty minutes. When they arrived at her hogan and unloaded the supplies, her grandfather informed them about a short-cut home. After being jostled around on the way there, they were ready for a different route.

Right before they pulled out, her grandfather threw an old broken handled shovel in the back of my parent's pickup truck and said, "You might need this." They didn't think much about it, until they started down the mountain. Much to their dismay, sections of the narrow road was washed out due to recent flooding. What a dilemma! They couldn't back up and they couldn't go forward. The mountain was on one side of the road and a dangerous drop off on the other. One wrong move would have forced them off the edge of the cliff.

Then my father remembered the broken shovel in the back of the truck and started building a road. He had to fill in the trenches with dirt that were three and four feet deep, then they would drive across to the other side. Dad was six foot three inches tall and weighed over two hundred pounds. He was solid muscle and strong as an ox. To give you an idea how strong, it was nothing for him to pick up the engine of a car, or set thirty foot utility poles in the ground by himself. He was a giant of a man in my little five foot two mother's eyes, especially that day. There were at least six different washed out areas in the one mile stretch down the mountain, so their fifteen minute shortcut ended up taking six hours. They left the girl's home at six o'clock and arrived at the mission at midnight.

This is my point. The elderly sometimes see themselves as that old rusty shovel that's been tossed aside. They feel useless, especially when they can't get a handle on the things they once gripped so tightly. It was a broken shovel that paved the way home for my parents. It's when the shovel was placed in my father's hands that the road was repaired. It's when we place our broken vessel into the strong hands of our Heavenly Father, that He's able to use us to rebuild lives and help them find their way back home.

And He said to me, "My grace is sufficient for you, for My strength is made perfect in weakness."   -**2 Corinthians 12:9**

We have great worth and we're always useful to Him, no matter how old we get. Have you priced antiques lately?

We have a quilt that my husband's grandma hand-stitched many years ago and we were careful not to use it, so it would stay protected and preserved. I found out that if you don't use it, the moth's will. I took it out of the linen closet and said, "Honey, your grandma would have been proud to know that her quilt not only kept her grandchildren warm, but her great and even great, great grandchildren as well. Do you know, that instead of wearing out, it has just become softer over time and use. Have you ever heard this statement? "You get softer with age, especially when it comes to grandchildren." I can sure vouch for that! Maybe it's because you don't have the full responsibility of raising them, and you have more time to really enjoy them. Your grandchildren still need you to cover them with your soft touch, love, and wisdom; which is what bridges the gap between generations.

A Grandmother's Love

Last week, I walked into a Goodwill store and noticed a young lady with green and black hair and piercings all over her face. She even had a green shirt on. I'm sure she didn't plan it that way, but it opened the door for me to strike up a conversation with her, so in a non-condemning way, I said, "Look at you, you're color coordinated." She smiled and said, "Yeah, I guess so." I found out that she was a single parent with a five year old son. After a bit of small talk, I said, "I have a scripture for you." She replied, "Oh you do?" You could tell that she had her guard up. As I began quoting the scripture, she looked completely stunned and her eyes filled with tears. Even though she claimed to be agnostic, she was amazed on how God's Word revealed exactly what she was going through. I walked around the racks of clothing where she was standing, and proceeded to minister with her.

After learning her name, I said, "Heather, God loves you and He desires to change your life and your present situation." She began to cry, then she showed me the scars on her wrist where she had tried to take her life. She had turned to a life of drugs and alcohol after her parents divorced. When they disconnected themselves from each other, she felt disconnected from life and didn't know who she was anymore. You could tell that she felt a little uncomfortable, but she agreed to let me pray with her. As soon as I held her hands to pray, she started trembling all over. The dam that contained her river of emotions had finally broken forth with tears of cleansing and release. Heather gave her life to the Lord, and for the first time she felt loved and totally free. Not only free, but joyful! She found herself laughing again, and she was long overdue for a good laugh. Especially since she had been lost in a deep dark depression. She walked in the Goodwill as an agnostic, and walked out a believer. Wow! Surprisingly, she said, "This is the first time anyone has ever witnessed to me." I felt so blessed!

What I find so interesting about this story is that her grandmother took her to church as a child. When she became a teenager, she got into the wrong crowd; therefore, it was very difficult for her grandmother to reach her. Instead of giving up, she continued to pray for her and started investing in Heather's five year old son, which was her great grandchild. She takes him to church and tells him all about Jesus. He loves going, and each service, he has requested prayer for his mother's salvation. He says, "Would you please pray that my mommy will get saved." Thanks be to God, he can finally feel secure, because his prayers have been answered! This has all been a result of a grandmother's love.

Virginia Marshall

Reflecting back on a recent Ladies Conference in Trinidad, I was very inspired by an eighty year old lady named Virginia Marshall, who went on the trip with us. She didn't just go along for the ride, she taught one of the seminars. She's a powerful woman of God, that gets around like she's forty. Everyone loves to be around her, not just because of her spiritual insight, but because of her humor. She's absolutely the life of the party. She was so cute. At the end of our trip, she looked at her daughter, Renee Clark, and said, "So when is our next event?" She's always raring to go somewhere.

Virginia became ill a few months ago, but instead of accepting defeat, she went into her den and began to pray. This was her prayer, "Dear God, I can't do what you have called me to do if I'm sick, so I need you to heal me now, so I can do your work." Well, she walked out of her den healed by the power of God and she spends every day working for the Lord. Whether it's in person or on the telephone, she's making a difference in someone's life. Her husband, Ervin, is eighty-three and is at their church every day making sure that everything's taken care of. They refuse to miss a golden opportunity, or to leave behind an unfinished task before the Lord calls them home.

Even to your old age, I am He, and even to gray hairs I will carry you! I have made, and I will bear; even I will carry, and will deliver you.   -Isaiah 46:4

Even if we're not as strong as we once were, and can't get around like we did before, there are still many ways to be used by God. Sending an encouraging card to someone can change their whole day and make them feel loved by Him. The telephone is another great witnessing tool! It's amazing how you're able to travel around the world without leaving your recliner. I cannot recall all the people that I've witnessed to on the telephone, including operators and business representatives. He will give us creative ways to reach out to others.

Elizabeth is eighty-three and still walking in her purpose. She buys dolls and stuffed animals from yard sales and Goodwill stores. She cleans them up and puts new clothes on them. She collects them throughout the year and then sends them with us to Mexico for our annual "Christmas On The Border" mission trip. Elizabeth has never been able to hand deliver her gifts, or even witness the joy on the children's faces as they embrace their new found friends; however, it gives her a great sense of fulfillment to know that she's touching a child through a simple act of kindness.

Honor widows, that are widows indeed.   -1 **Timothy 5:3 (KJV)**

Honor in this scripture means: to value.

When their spouse is no longer living, and their children live far away, they feel all alone and unvalued. Can I get a little personal? Even as children, we can neglect and take for granted the people that we love the most. The cares of life can cause us to be too busy for the ones that really matter to us. We may not be able to visit our parents daily, but we can call them. They just need to hear our voice, and know they're still loved and needed.

A couple in our church named, Juan and Debbie Solis, determined to make a difference in the life of their neighbor, Joann, who was well into her eighties. She didn't have children or any other living relatives, so they have made her feel like part of their family. They've taken care of her as if she was their own mother. She does-n't drive, so her life has only consisted of her city. One of her dreams was to see the Arch in St. Louis, Missouri, which is one hundred and fifty miles away from her home. Debbie made that dream a reality by taking her there, and many other places that she's desired to go. Joann said that she just started living when they came into her life.

Debbie was also responsible for giving an eighty year old man his first birthday party. She secretly called all his friends and family to participate in what would be the ultimate surprise of his life. The room was decorated with balloons, streamers, and with all the people he loved. They blind-folded him, led him into the party, and then they took the cloth off of his eyes. When he saw his cake lit with candles and all the familiar faces, he put his hands over his

face and started crying. As they sang the birthday chorus, he felt
so honored and overwhelmed that he could barely talk. What a way
to demonstrate the love of God and to bring value to others!

Another lady we know named Tammy, has a real heart for the
elderly. She looks out for her senior neighbors, spends time with
them, and prays with them regularly. Not long ago, her neighbor
fell and injured her head pretty badly, and instead of pushing her
Life Alert button, she crawled to the phone to call Tammy. When
Tammy arrived, she ask her why she didn't push the button for
medical response. She said, "Because I can always depend on you
to be here first, besides, you are my caregiver."

*Therefore, as we have opportunity, let us do good to all, especially
to those who are of the household of faith.*   - **Galatians 6:10**

Remember, these are the "Golden Years," not the "Olden Years."
As we know, before gold can be classified as the purest, most trea-
sured metal, it must first be tried with fire. Think about it, we
haven't gone through the fire and years of refinement for nothing.
This should be the brightest time of our lives. Gold resist rust, and
so should we. We are considered valuable to God, a peculiar treasure, and our faith is much more precious than gold.

*That the trial of your faith, being much more precious than of gold
that perisheth, though it be tried with fire, might be found unto*

praise and honour and glory at the appearing of Jesus Christ.
-1 Peter 1:7 (KJV)

Let's walk in the reflection of His love, until we walk on streets of gold!

How can we encourage the elderly? Send a card, give them a call, or just drop by and give them a hug. We can make them feel loved, useful, needed, and valued once again.

10

YOU'RE CLEAN, EXCEPT YOUR FEET

The Lord has led me to literally hundreds of people throughout all different venues and statuses of life, and there's something I've found that most of them have in common. They are struggling to let go of the past. This is not only true for sinners, but also numerous Christians as well. Several years ago, I was drawn to these scriptures and felt the unction to memorize them.

Remember ye not the former things, neither consider the things of old. Behold, I will do a new thing; now it shall spring forth; shall ye not know it? I will even make a way in the wilderness, and rivers in the desert. -**Isaiah 43:18-19 (KJV)**

There is something that happens when you speak the Word of God over someone. It's in this moment that our witnessing moves to ministering, and it becomes His words and not our own. We are just mail carriers who deliver His love letter to the world. On a regular basis, God will prompt me to give a scripture to an individual, and I've watched their countenance change as tears began to flow down their face. Often times they don't know what they're experiencing, they just know that they feel a sense of peace along with a warm sensation flowing through their body. His Word is alive, powerful, and sharper than any two-edged sword. One side of the sword cuts out the things that don't belong in us, and the other side is like a surgical instrument that skillfully administers healing. I have watched these scriptures break the chains of the past, give strength to the weak, and bring salvation to the lost. It's not to say that these are the only life changing verses; as a matter of fact, I write others down on a ministry card for them as well. However, Isaiah 43:18-19 helps them close the door to their past, so they can embrace the new things that God has for them. Let's break this scripture down in its original Hebrew text.

1.) Remember not means: Don't mention it, think about it, or keep record of it

2.) Former things means: The past

3.) Consider means: To separate mentally

4.) New thing means: Fresh, or come into being

Basically to experience the new, we have to release the old. How is this possible?

We must first FORGIVE. That's a big word, and it's not easy for any of us to swallow. Not only for sinners, but Christians alike. Yes, that's right, even Christians are faced with certain obstacles that make it challenging to forgive; but in order to walk in peace and experience new heights with God, it's imperative! Let's see how Jesus demonstrates the power of forgiveness in John Chapter 13.

The day before the Passover Festival, Jesus knew that the hour had come for him to leave this world, so he gathered his disciples together for an evening meal. After supper, he got up from the table, took off his outer garment, and tied a towel around his waist. He then poured water into a basin and proceeded to wash and dry the disciples' feet.

Everyone is taken back; they're quite embarrassed and humbled to say the least. I can just hear their thoughts. "We forgot to hire a servant!" Washing the guest's feet was reserved for the servant of the house, and not just any servant, but the one with the least seniority.

Can you imagine running into Bill Gates as you were leaving the restroom? That may not be out of the ordinary, but what if you had to hold the door open for him so he could roll in his mop bucket to clean up after you. You may think to yourself, "That's the janitor's job!" Sure he could have started out in that position, but he worked his way up. Jesus didn't work his way up, he worked his way down and became a servant to all. He intended to teach his disciples a valuable lesson on humility and forgiveness that they would never forget. When he got ready to wash Peter's feet, Peter boldly said what everyone else was thinking, "Are you going to wash my feet, Lord?" Jesus said, "You may not understand what I'm doing now, but you will later."

Peter said, "You will never wash my feet!" Then Jesus said, "If I do not wash your feet, you will have no part with me." Peter's response was, "Not only my feet, but my hands and my head also." Jesus stated, "He that is bathed, only needs to wash his feet." In other words, "You're clean, except your feet." You see, the Lord knew the path that Peter would take, that's why he needed to wash his feet. Peter was so confident in his relationship with Jesus, that he actually believed he would lay his life down for him; but Jesus knew that Peter would deny him on three different occasions.

After the Sanhedrin police force arrested the Lord, Peter got scared and ran. Then he was recognized by others, so he denied the fact that he even knew him. After Jesus was crucified, Peter wept bitterly. He was overcome with so much guilt that he was too ashamed to even congregate with the other disciples. Who amongst us hasn't felt like Peter? We love God and feel sure that we're rooted, grounded, and steadfast in our walk with Him, but then something happens and we find our feet dirty from the path we've taken. We've spoken words that we wish somehow we could take back, or perhaps we've left someone out in the cold that really needed us to cover them. Maybe it was what someone did or said to us. If we dwell on it, our hurt turns to anger, and our resentment and anguish turns to bitterness and unforgiveness.

Do you know that after many years of study, medical professionals have discovered that the emotional stress of bitterness, long term grief, and unforgiveness will release deadly toxins in our body? Over time, this creates the right climate for arthritis, cancer, and ulcers to thrive. Of course, these are not the only causes of these diseases, but such harbored emotions can have a devastating effect on us; not only spiritually, but physically as well.

God desires to do a new thing in us, but once again, before we can experience the new, we must release the old.

Face To Face

In 1972, my maternal grandmother purchased a fairly large church building in Blodgett, Missouri. It was built in 1929, but was filled with a great deal of character. It had gorgeous stained glass windows, beautiful woodwork, and an ornate ceiling that was seventeen feet tall. She had high hopes that my father would grasp the vision and pastor the church, but at the time, he didn't share the same sentiment. He was still recouping from the last church she had handed over to him. You see, after she returned from the mission field in New Mexico, she was asked to serve as an interim pastor at a church in Wisconsin. It was not an appealing offer, especially since the congregation was in a heated battle of strife and confusion. To give you an idea just how far the people had digressed, two elders got on either side of the pastor, physically picked him up, and escorted him out of the front door of the Sanctuary. It obviously wasn't a very desirable mission, unless you undeniably had a mandate from God. Well, after grandma's earnest prayer for reinforcements, dad finally took on the challenge.

For the next year, he taught them how to walk in God's love and forgiveness. As a result, lives were changed and hearts were reunited. When my parent's work was over in Wisconsin, the members of the church were saddened, but they passed the baton to another pastor that would lead them to the next level.

After they moved to Missouri where my father was raised, he became an associate pastor in a neighboring town and was pretty comfortable with that position; but my grandmother was a very ambitious woman with a lot of zeal. I guess she felt like her son-in-law needed a little extra push. So as before, her and my mother began to pray. At first he turned down her offer in Blodgett, but once again, the Lord began to deal with his heart. However, right before he was installed as pastor, he had to confront some deep rooted bitterness from the past.

One Sunday night before service, an elderly man walked in the church with his wife and five grown children. Of course, we were always delighted for new people to come. So without delay, my father went back to greet them. While dad cordially shook the old man's hand, he asked him his name and as he identified himself, my father's face turned pale. It just so happened to be the man that he had grown up to hate. He was responsible for assaulting two of my dad's uncles; killing one and shooting part of the face off of the other.

In the Spring of 1941, Central America experienced heavy rains which resulted in some major flooding. Crops were damaged and homes were threatened to be ruined. The old man was a cantankerous farmer who owned quite a bit of land, so when water began to rise on his fields, he hired men to dig ditches. In the process, he took the liberty to have trenches dug out in front of homes that were near his property. This was all done without the consent of any homeowners, and my uncle's house was one of them.

As they came in from their place of employment, they couldn't get into their driveway. So they immediately got out their shovels and started filling the trenches with dirt that the ditch diggers left behind. Shortly after, the man came by in his car and angrily said, "Lay your shovels down!" They didn't heed warning, consequently, he pulled out a double barrel shotgun and killed dad's uncle right in front of his family. Then he shot the other one in the face. He was bleeding profusely, but he found enough strength to drag himself to the house. Suddenly, his wife bolted out of the front door with a gun and clumsily took a shot at the farmer as he was driving away. What a tragedy! This calamity was heartrending enough, but to make matters more distressing, the farmer was never convicted. Because of his involvement in politics, he had friends in high places; therefore, it was nothing more than a mock trial. He told the judge that this woman just started shooting at him; therefore, the case was ruled as self defense and justice was never served. From that day forward the Russell brothers vowed to take revenge. My father was six years old at the time, but remembers it vividly. He was raised to detest this man. Even hearing the farmer's name, would cause the family's blood to boil.

Now, over thirty years later, the farmer comes to the church that my father is getting ready to pastor. "What's he want?" "Does he know who I am?" "What if my family finds out?" All this is running through dad's mind and it's more than he can take. So with no explanation, he went home trying to escape the wounds from long ago. He thought, "Surely I'll never see him again," but when he drove into the church parking lot the next Sunday, the man's car was there. Dad dreadfully went inside, and tried to cover his animosity toward him. As a little girl, I remember hearing my dad whisper to my grandmother, "That man over there is a murderer!" "He killed my uncle!" My grandma's response was, "Well, then he sure needs God." She reminded him that the farmer was in the right place to receive Him. That wasn't what dad wanted to hear at the time, but God began to prick his heart and reminded him of the scripture: *"Whoever hates his brother, is a murderer...* -1John 3:15

Even though this man wasn't his brother in the Lord, he realized that the hate he had toward him was equal to the murder that this man had committed. So he made his way back to the farmer and his family once again, and welcomed them.

Each time he made the effort to shake the man's hand, the love of God would humble his heart and before long, he found the compassion to forgive. Eventually, nearly all of that family received salvation and became some of the most faithful members of the church. Dad ended up traveling over a hundred miles to preach his wife's funeral. Finally, he was called to the hospital to pray for the old man in his final hours.

For You, Lord, are good, and ready to forgive, and abundant in mercy to all those who call upon You.   **-Psalm 86:5**

It would be easy to figure that the farmer got off scot-free, but did he really? We know an individual who killed someone in self defense, and he said he relives the incident every single day of his life. Even though physical bars do not hold him, he's tormented with guilt in the prison of his mind continually. Can you imagine someone who purposely murdered someone? They're haunted by the ghosts of their past, paralyzed by fear, and driven to substance abuse; but God still loves them and desires to soften their stony heart.

Even though the old man supposed he was doomed for hell, he

brought his family to church in hopes that they would have a chance at heaven. However, God showed him mercy during the last moments of his life.

What I want to point out is, before my father could experience the most rewarding assignment in his ministry, he was required to come face to face with his past. Little did he know, that over the next forty-five years, the Lord would use him to raise up pastors, evangelists, and missionaries for the glory of God; but first he needed to forgive. Just as Jesus washed Peter's feet, my dad was compelled to wash the feet of his offender.

Forgiveness Is Not An Emotion

In 1941, Corrie Ten Boom and her sister, Betsie, helped many Jews escape the Nazis during World War II. They built a secret room in their home in Holland to hide and protect the Jews until they could find a safe escape. In 1944, a Dutchman came into their home and asked for money so he could help save some Jews. It turned out that he was working for the Germans, so her and Betsie were caught, beaten, and taken to prison. For four months, Corrie lived alone in a cold, dark cell without a bed. There was only a dirty, straw mattress with one blanket that the previous prisoner had gotten sick on. She was given a plate of thin porridge in the morning and a piece of black bread in the evening. During that time, she became very ill, so they sent her to the hospital. Before she was discharged, a nurse hid hygiene items, vitamin drops, and most importantly, a booklet of the four gospels in her clothes.

She was released from prison and was sent to a concentration camp in Ravensbruck, Germany, where she was reunited with her sister, but it was far worse than the prison. Fourteen hundred women were packed like cattle into a barrack room that was built to house 400 people. They had to sleep on straw mattresses that were saturated with dust and infested with fleas. Every morning during roll call, 35,000 names were called and if they didn't stand up straight enough, they were beaten with riding whips. They were only given enough food to stay alive. Many of the women became weak and very ill, so Corrie gave them some of her vitamin drops which would help to revive them. Mysteriously, the little bottle of drops lasted for months, much like the widow's cruse of oil from the Bible. In spite of the hardship and brutal conditions, Corrie and Betsie secretly had Bible studies with the other women from the booklet of the four gospels that the nurse had given Corrie in the hospital. Hundreds got saved! After a while they began to thank God for the fleas, because at least it kept the guards from making their regular rounds.

One day while Corrie and Betsie were lifting heavy beams of steel, Betsie fell beneath the load. A guard accused her of being lazy and started beating her mercilessly. In so much, that she was hospitalized. As a result, she died. Corrie felt abandoned by God, heartbroken, and all alone. Then she remembered how Betsie refused to give in to hatred. Even while the guard was beating her, she was praying for him. She did not give the enemy power over her mind or her spirit.

A few days after Betsie's death, Corrie's name was called. She didn't know if she was getting ready to be shot or taken to the gas chamber. Surprisingly, she was dismissed and sent back to her home in Holland. She found out later that her dismissal was a mistake. One week after her release, all the women her age were killed. She began to thank God for her rescue. After the War was over, Corrie was free to share her testimony with others. She was invited to speak in many churches throughout her region.

Three years after her release, in the year of 1947, she came back to Germany with a message that God truly forgives; but she was faced with one of the hardest test of her faith. While she was ministering at a church in Munich, Germany, she saw a heavy set man in a gray overcoat with a brown felt hat clutched between his hands. As people were filing out of the basement where she had spoken, he began to work his way up to the front where she was. In her book "I'm Still Learning To Forgive," Corrie said, "One moment I saw the overcoat and the brown hat; the next, a blue uniform and a visored cap with its skull and crossbones. It came back with a rush: the huge room with its harsh overhead lights, and pathetic pile of dresses and shoes in the center of the floor. Then I remembered the shame of walking naked past this man. I could see my sister's frail form ahead of me with her sharp ribs beneath the parchment skin."

Her heart began to race, but she tried to keep her composure. He said, "You mentioned Ravensbruck in your talk. I was a guard there, but since that time I have become a Christian. I know that God has forgiven me for the cruel things I did there, but I would like to hear it from your lips as well." With his hand extended he said, "Will you forgive me?" She said, "I stood there, my sins had been forgiven, yet I could not forgive. Betsie had died in that place! Could he erase her slow, terrible death, simply for the asking?" Corrie expressed, "It could not have been many seconds that he stood there with his hand held out, but to me it seemed like hours, as I wrestled with the most difficult thing I ever had to do. For I had to do it! I knew that! The message that God forgives has a prior condition, that we forgive those who have injured us." She was then reminded of this scripture:

"But if you do not forgive men their trespasses, neither will your Father forgive your trespasses."   -**Matthew 6:15**

Corrie proceeded, "And yet I stood there with coldness clutching my heart, but forgiveness is not an emotion. I knew that too! Forgiveness is an act of the will, and the will can function regardless of the temperature of the heart."

"Jesus, help me!" I prayed silently. "I can lift my hand, I can do that much. You supply the feeling. Then, so woodenly, mechanically, I thrust my hand into the one stretched out to me, and as I did an incredible thing took place." She said, "The current started in my shoulder, raced down my arm, and sprang into our joined hands. Then this healing warmth seemed to flood my whole being, bringing tears to my eyes." I cried, "I forgive you, brother, with all of my heart!"

She said, "For a long moment we grasped each other's hands; the former guard and the former prisoner, and I had never known God's love so intensely as I did then."

Like my father, Corrie thought she had forgiven everyone in her life, until she had to come face to face with her opponent. You see, God wanted to take her ministry to a whole new dimension, but in order to really teach on the power of forgiveness, she needed to truly forgive. After her willingness to forgive, God took her message and ministry around the world.

Forgiveness is not something that comes natural for any of us. It's first a choice, then a simple act of obedience.

After Jesus was resurrected, he instructed the two Marys to tell his disciples and Peter that he would meet them in Galilee, just as he told them he would. He made it a point to mention Peter's name, because he knew how broken he was. His heart was still devastated from his failure, so Jesus wanted to make sure that he knew he had forgiven him and that he had included him with the others.

The message he was trying to get across to the disciples was: I'm cleansing your path, and I'm forgiving you even before you hurt me; so just as I have forgiven you, likewise, forgive others and forgive yourselves.

How could Jesus forgive his disciples and ultimately the world? I believe the answer is in this text:

Now before the Feast of the Passover, when Jesus knew that His hour had come that He should depart from this world to the Father, having loved His own who were in the world, He loved them to the end.
-John 13:1

The answer is LOVE. He could forgive, because he loved them. We must cry out, "Lord, perfect me in your love and let me see others, as you see them."

Just as Jesus had washed Peter's feet, he desires to wash ours. Take a moment, close your eyes, and imagine Jesus washing your feet.

Now speak the names out that have hurt you, and from a sincere heart, repeat this prayer:

"Dear Lord, I release the hurts of these people from my heart, and today, I choose to forgive them; even as You have forgiven me from all my sins. I ask that You would remove any root of bitterness and never let it return. I bring every thought under subjection and I make a new commitment to serve You all the days of my life . Please, live in my heart, use me for Your glory, and love the world through me. I love You, Father, and I will forever be Your child. In Jesus' Name, I pray, amen.

Now, take a deep breath, and from your heart release any negative residue that may have remained. Do it three times to signify resurrection power. Once again, close your eyes and lift up your hands. Now breathe in the breath of God. Envision it being the actual breath of your Heavenly Father. Do you feel Him? Now relax in His presence, wrap your arms around yourself, and let Him love on you. Listen now for His words of peace.

You will keep him in perfect peace, whose mind is stayed on You, because he trusts in You.   **-Isaiah 26:3**

"Peace I leave with you, My peace I give to you; not as the world gives do I give to you. Let not your heart be troubled, neither let it be afraid."   **-John 14:27**

And the peace of God, which surpasses all understanding, will guard your hearts and minds through Christ Jesus.   **-Philippians 4:7**

Now may the Lord of peace Himself give you peace always in every way. The Lord be with you all.   **-2 Thessalonians 3:16**

Therefore, if anyone is in Christ, he is a new creation; old things have passed away; behold, all things have become new. Now all things are of God, who has reconciled us to Himself through Jesus Christ, and has given us the ministry of reconciliation.

-2 Corinthians 5:17-18

11

SEVEN EFFECTIVE WAYS
TO WITNESS

Is there a certain method or secret formula to witnessing? What do we say? Do we approach people with words like, "Do you know Jesus?" or "If you died today, would you go to Heaven or Hell?" These phrases may work for some, but in most cases, folks get offended by it; therefore, we don't feel accepted or very well received. Then what penetrates the walls of their hearts, which ultimately leads them to Christ?

A couple of years ago, a pastor friend of ours, Glynn Davis, ask me to teach a class on witnessing. As I was praying for wisdom and direction, the Lord began to show me an acronym for the word witness. I discovered within this word, seven practical, yet very effective ways to witness. Let's begin.

1.) The W In Witness Stands For WARM

One of the meanings of warm is to inspire with a kindly feeling, and one of the illustrations given in the dictionary is a smile. Have you ever heard the phrase, "Your smile melted my heart?" When you smile at someone, you're making them feel warm. Remember, we must RECOVER them. A smile is the universal language that we all understand. It's catchy and I like to spread it around. It's an automatic response for me. Nothing forced, plastic, or phony; it's a true reflection of His joy in my heart. No matter what you're facing, there's always something to smile about.

Remember the song from Sunday School class, "Oh let the sun shine in, face it with a grin, smiler's never lose and frowners never win, so open up your heart and let the sun shine in." A smile allows the "Son" of God to shine on their gloomy day and on their present circumstance. It spreads happiness. I love to make people smile, especially those who are grumpy, or disheartened. A smile can even warm the coldest heart.

Years ago, my sister, Becky, and I were in line at a drive through bank. When we approached the window, the teller said, "I've just got to ask you ladies something. Every time I see you, you're always smiling and I just want to know, what makes you so happy?" Of course, it opened the door for us to witness.

One smile was worth millions to one young lady. On a cool autumn afternoon, an elderly gentlemen walked very gingerly with his head hung down. Many of his friends and loved ones had passed away and he felt all alone. He found his place on a nearby park bench to do some deep thinking and soul searching. About that time, a lady and her little girl walked by. The little girl caught his eye, as she gave him a smile from ear to ear. It warmed his heart so much that it gave him a reason to live and he never forgot it. Years later, when he died, he had willed all his fortune to her.

A smile is a very effective communication tool that has the potential to disarm those standing firmly on guard, and cause them to be at ease. It not only brings you on common ground together, but it says, "I'm approachable." Our smile is the open door of interaction. Have you ever noticed that the phrase, "Hi, how are you doing," usually comes out of our mouth right after we've smiled at someone? One smile has the capability to resolve conflict and it says, "It's going to be alright."

A few years back, Rick and I were invited to a conference in Dallas, Texas. Our hotel was only a mile or so from a fairly large shopping mall, so after we settled into our room, I went to see if I could sniff out some good deals. I discovered that everything really is bigger in Texas. It took longer than I expected to get from one store to the next, so before I realized it, I had to leave to get ready for church. I usually always have a witnessing opportunity while I'm shopping, but not today. All I had time to do was smile at a Dillard's employee, as I scurried past her to the nearest exit.

Two days later, I returned back to the mall, but this time I made sure I allowed for more time to shop. Once again I ended up at Dillards, and as always, my attention was drawn to the group of crowded clearance racks. As I draped a few items across my arm, an employee said, "Would you like me to hold these for you, until you're ready to try them on?" I said, "Sure, Thank you!" As I glanced at her eyes, the Lord began to deal with me to witness to her. I stopped what I was doing and said, "I have a scripture for you today," She said, "Really?" When I began quoting the scripture, she began to cry. Then she proceeded to explain. "You see, I've not been in the United States very long. I'm from Africa. My husband left me because I was pregnant. The fact is, she is his daughter, but he just didn't want the responsibility of another child. I have felt completely abandoned and alone."

I ministered with her and began to speak wholeness and peace into her life. She took two steps back and looked at me with widened eyes. She said, "Were you in here two days ago?" Before I could answer her, she began to describe the outfit I was wearing at the time. I said, "Yes, as a matter of fact I was." Then she said, "When you walked past me, something went all through my body and I have not been able to get your face out of my mind." She started to cry again, because she knew God sent one of His messengers her way to affirm His love to her. Wow! I had no idea she was the woman I smiled at as I was rushing out of the mall two days prior. The Lord was preparing her heart so I could minister to her.

But we have this treasure in earthen vessels, that the excellence of the power may be of God and not of us. -**2 Corinthians 4:7**

We are simply clay pots that carry His presence.

But how can one be warm alone? -**Ecclesiastes 4:11**

RECOVER them with a smile. Our smile is the key that unlocks the door of witnessing.

Remember, if someone doesn't have a smile, give them one of yours.

2.) The I In Witness Stands For INTERESTED

...look out not only for his onw interests, but also for the interests of others. -**Philippians 2:4**

The word interest in Webster's Dictionary means: to engage or take a share or concern in. I find it interesting that on the top ten list of things that are hard to start, conversation rates third. I thought it to be kind of funny that it placed, just below a lawn mower. That's why I believe God gives us creative ways to engage someone in conversation. You may have to crank it more than once, but after a few tries you'll be in full throttle.

One way is to compliment them, or comment on something that

stands out to you. For instance, recently, while I was in the ladies restroom at a gas station, I noticed a lady with beautiful green eyes. So while we were washing our hands I said, "You have pretty eyes." A big grin came across her face as she thanked me for the compliment. Then she told me that she inherited them from her father's side. A conversation begin to brew. Then, well you know what happened next. I gave her a scripture and she began to cry right there in the ladies restroom. It all started with a compliment. It's showing an interest in someone else and making them feel special.

Have you ever talked with someone and the topic was all about them, whether it was all about their interest, business or ministry? The exchange becomes all one-sided and a little out of balance. I don't approach someone and began telling them all about our ministry, and my life's history. My interest is focused on them at the moment. As a matter of fact, sometimes they find out my name after they've accepted Jesus into their life; because it's simply not about me.

Slip Sliding Away

When Bethany was six years old and Jonathan was four, we were called upon to minister at a state conference in Iuka, Mississippi. On our way there, it began to rain very heavily and visibility was very poor. Rick sensed that we took the wrong exit, so he turned at the first road to the right to get back on track. In the process of turning around, he dropped the right front wheel off a concrete embankment. Suddenly, we felt the car shift sideways. I said, "Rick, stop, we're sliding!"

We were in the middle of nowhere. It was dark and pouring down rain. Fortunately, there was a greasy spoon restaurant just across the street. Rick said, "You guys stay here while I see if I can get someone to pull us out." After he crossed the street, Bethany wouldn't get back into the car. She started to cry when I tried to coach her to get back in. She was obviously afraid that the car would flip over. Jonathan was a little concerned, but he kept comforting his big sister. I said, "Sissy, let's just pray to Jesus, and it'll be alright." With tears coming down her cheeks she replied, "I think He's sleeping." Then I decided to take the kids and walk across the street to the restaurant. What I didn't realize was while Bethany was leaning against the car door, she accidently hit the lock button, so now the keys are locked inside the car and it's running. When it rains, it pours.

When I located Rick in his pursuit to find a chain, I told him of our new dilemma, so he looks at the guy in the restaurant that owned a towing service and said, "Let's go get your wrecker." The man pulls up in a brand new tow truck. Right about this time, you can imagine what Rick's thinking, "I'm getting ready to make a payment on this rig!"

Our waitress seemed curious, so I informed her about our situation. When I told her we were on our way to church, she looked down and said, "I used to go to church." At that moment, I knew exactly why we were there. She was away from God and needed to know that He still loved her and was calling her back to Him. Tears filled her eyes as she felt His embrace once again.

While we finally got back on the road, I noticed that Rick was quiet. I knew he was just trying to make sense of it all, so I broke the silence by saying, "You know while you were getting the car out of the ditch, I got to lead a lady back to the Lord." He hit the steering wheel and said, "That's it! That's why all this happened!" You could tell he was feeling better about all the trouble he had just gone through, especially if it was for a lost soul.

I'll never forget Rick walking up to the pulpit that night with mud all over his suit, and it was easy to see that the congregation was curiously anxious to hear his story. He proceeded, "Well, what I thought was the wrong road, and the wrong place, turned out to be the right place at just the right time for someone to find the Lord."

This is my point, when I sensed the drawing to witness to the waitress, I found myself looking out for her interest instead of my own; therefore, it didn't matter what was going on in my life at the present time, because I just knew that God was going to work it all for good.

3.) The T In Witness Stands For TOUCHABLE

And He put forth His hand, and touched him... -Luke 5:13 (KJV)

Miami's Touch Research Institute says: Without appropriate touch, people cannot grow and develop properly. Touch is powerful. They've discovered that the touch is the greatest sense in our body. Our skin, which is the largest organ, contains thousands of sensory receptors. When we're touched, endorphins are released in our body, which aids in healing.

Do you remember the story of the leper in Luke chapter five? He urgently requested Jesus to heal him. He said, "If you will, you can make me clean." Jesus said, "I will!" Instead of just speaking the word, Jesus reached out and touched him.

The Lord knew that he needed more than a word, he needed His touch. Like the leper, patients with highly contagious conditions who are denied skin contact find it more distressing than the symptoms of the illness.

There is a true story documented from Lactation Education about a baby boy that was born with a rare stomach disease. Struggling to breathe on his own, he was immediately placed on life support. After a few hours, they determined that he was clinically dead. So the parents made the dreadful decision to remove life support, but not before the mother could hold him for the very first time.

Suddenly, while she cuddled him against her skin, life started to come back into his tiny body. His bluish green flesh began to turn red and finally a soft pink color, as his vital signs returned to normal. They were all wonderfully amazed. It was a miracle, and the power of skin to skin contact.

On one of our missionary journeys to Trinidad, Hannah, a young woman in her early twenties was visiting from Chile. She was staying with the native pastor and his family. She had already been in Trinidad for two months and still had one more month to go. After I had the opportunity to minister with her, I gave her a warm hug and said, "This is a hug from your momma." For some reason, it just came out of my mouth. After I said that, she melted in my arms and started crying. She said, "Right before you came, I said, God, I just need a hug from my momma."

There was another lady that had gone through many tragedies. One of her sons was run over by a car, and the other was hit while riding his bicycle, leaving him crippled for life. Several years later she lost her husband. Not able to cope with the grief, she isolated herself for months. Finally, through much encouragement from others, she went to church. Longing for the embrace of her Heavenly Father, she looked for the biggest man she could find to give her a hug. It happened to be her best friend's husband, Doug. There are times in our life when we just need a Doug hug.

After you've witnessed to someone, shake their hand, give them a hug. It makes them feel loved and connected with the family of

God. He desires to hug them through us.

In Luke chapter seven we learn about the woman that washed Jesus' feet with her tears and dried them with her hair. The Pharisee despised the woman because of her past, so he thought within his heart, *"If this man was a prophet, he would know what kind of woman this was touching him."* He was right about one thing, she was touching Jesus; but not only His feet, her worship touched His heart.

Touch in the Greek means: to join, start a fire, and to leave part of one's self behind.

You see, the touch of someone's hand or embrace signifies care and comfort, telling us that we're not alone. It touches God when we touch each other.

4. The N In Witness Stands For NICE

And be kind to one another....   -Ephesians 4:32

Nice means: to be kind, polite and agreeable.

A couple of years ago, Rick and I were at a Cracker Barrel. As soon as we placed our order, I noticed a lady sitting alone at the table next to us. Well, as you can imagine, I engaged her in a conversation. When I told her where we were from, she asked what we did for a living, so I told her a little about our ministry. She was interested since she also traveled extensively delivering donor organs to medical facilities. When we got ready to leave, I gave her a word of encouragement and handed her a card with scriptures on the back of it. Fighting back the tears, she said, "I'm agnostic, but there's just something different about you two, so I'm going to read these verses you gave me."

When she made me aware that she was not a believer, I just continued to be nice to her. We don't have to be intimidated when someone doesn't accept our God. We can just choose not to be disagreeable, condemning, or argumentative. His Word will always stand for itself and is able to penetrate the toughest heart.

"It's nice to be important, but it's more important to be nice."

-Author Unknown

5.) The E In Witness Stands For ENTHUSIASTIC

He gave Himself for us to set us free from every sin and to cleanse us so that we can be His special people who are enthusiastic about doing good things.   **-Titus 2:14 (GWT)**

The word enthusiastic simply means: to show great excitement toward an interest.

In other words, the zeal you feel on the inside is making its way to the outside and people are drawn to you, simply because you produce synergy.

Now on the other hand, if someone was trying to sell you something, and was apathetic about his product, you would probably think that he really doesn't believe in it, so why should you? Of course, I'm not implying that we should be over zealous, or fanatical. That tends to make people feel nervous and want to get away from us as quickly as they can.

The reason hundreds of people have gone on mission trips with us over the years is because they felt our enthusiasm and the passion in our hearts; therefore, they were eager to join the team. We all know that you experience more excitement when you're at a ballgame, than when you're watching it on television. Let the joy of the Lord overflow on to others you meet. They'll not only be inspired, they'll want what you have.

Enthusiasm is contagious, be a carrier.

-Susan Rabin

6.) The S In Witness Stands For SINCERE

That ye may approve the things that are excellent, that ye may be sincere and without offense till the day of Christ...

-**Philippians 1:10**

To be sincere means: to be open, devout, heartfelt, and real. The Greek definition means: without deceit, tested to be genuine and judged by sunlight.

During Apostle Paul's day, most of the merchants would sell their items on the street, much like our flea markets today. Often times pottery would be displayed under tents or beneath some sort of awning. If the buyer was interested in a particular piece, they would ask the store attendant if they could take the pottery out into the sunlight so they could hold it up, revealing any crack. That's where the phrase, judged by sunlight, came from.

Whether we realize it or not, people are testing us to see if we're really genuine. If we're not whole, it will seep through the cracks in our lives. People know if we actually care, not by our religious jargon, but our authenticity. In my southern Missouri drawl, just be your real self.

7.) The S In Witness Stands For STRONG

Have I not commanded you? Be strong and courageous. Do not be afraid; do not be discouraged, for the Lord your God will be with you wherever you go.... -**Joshua 1:9 (NIV)**

Strong means: to have strength or power greater than average.

These are the individuals with bold courage. They refuse to give in to pressure, or give up when the going gets tough. Are some people just born with this type of quality? No, it comes through the power of the Holy Spirit. The Lord instructed the disciples.

But you shall receive power when the Holy Spirit has come upon you; and you shall be witnesses to Me...   **-Acts 1:8**

You may be saying, "I've received the Holy Spirit, but I don't always feel very strong or powerful." It's kind of like a lamp. As long as it's plugged into the main source, you can access it whenever you need the light.

Holy Boldness

A few years ago on our way home from Texas, we stopped at a service station to fuel up the car. When I went into the ladies restroom, I noticed a lady freshening up at the vanity. She was fairly tall, with fire engine red hair. Her attire was shorts and a tank top, which exhibited her bulging muscles. As you can envision, she looked rather intimidating.

When I got ready to leave the restroom she was still there. I walked out, but the very moment the door swung behind me, I felt the prompting of the Lord to go back in and witness to her. When I grabbed the door handle, a holy boldness came over me. I walked right up to her and said, "The Lord has just dealt with me to minister with you." She looked at me a little stunned. You could tell that I caught her completely off guard.

I proceeded, "I have a scripture for you." In her low voice, she said, "Okay." As I began to quote His Word to her, that tough exterior suddenly began to soften. The tears streamed down her face as she wept. I said, "Someone's been praying for you." She responded, "It's my aunt!" It turns out that she was a truck driver with her life on the run. Years of drugs, failed marriages, and endless heartbreak had taken its toll, and she was finally ready for change. While she was still weeping, I led her through the prayer of salvation. What a transformation! I hugged her and she cried some more, but now it was tears of joy.

I can just imagine what people were thinking who were coming in and out of the restroom. Here I am hugged up with this woman who looked like a wrestler. I'm sure it looked kind of odd, but at that moment, it really didn't matter what anyone thought, nor was I ashamed of the Gospel that had just changed this woman's life.

For the eyes of the Lord run to and fro throughout the whole earth, to show Himself strong on behalf of those whose heart is loyal to Him......   -**2 Chronicles 16:9**

If I had looked at my fleshly strength compared to the muscular woman in the restroom, I wouldn't have stood a chance. But when I chose to be available and obedient, His strength was made perfect through my weakness. He's looking for those who are humble and fully committed, that He can show Himself strong through.

Remember Peter in the Bible? He was known to get his foot stuck in his mouth on many different occasions, but when he received the Holy Spirit, a boldness came over him and he spoke as one having authority; therefore, thousands were saved.

I have watched the Lord use these seven handy tools to reconstruct many lives. He is the Master Builder! He'll do great things through us, as we remain willing and ready at all times.

12

STAY READY

Minutemen were volunteer soldiers from the Revolutionary War era who worked jobs, but stood ready and available at a minute's notice. Just like minutemen, we should stay prepared at all times. We never know when He's going call upon us to serve. Whether it's keeping the enemy at bay, or pulling the wounded from the gutter; we must be among the first to volunteer, whatever our assignment might be.

Therefore, you also be ready.......   -**Matthew 24:44**

How do you stay ready? Before I'm ready to face the world, I get on my face, before the Lord. I'm not referring to a routine of religious calisthenics. I have discovered that daily communion with our Heavenly Father, is what builds a healthy relationship, and a steady diet of His Word is essential for spiritual growth and fitness.

Right Up Front

Two years ago, I was checking for certain items at a Sears department store. While I was walking down the front aisle, an employee asked me if I needed help finding something.

She shared with me later, that she thought within herself, "This woman can help me." I paused and said, "Yes as a matter of fact you can, I have a scripture for you." Now we are standing by a display at the front entrance of the store. Of course, I had no idea what was getting ready to take place. What God was about to do was not hidden in a corner somewhere, it was right up front.

Without making a scene, I quoted the scripture and ministered with her briefly, but as soon as I took her hand and began to pray with her, she dropped to the floor and started crying OUT LOUD. Then it happened! She began speaking in a heavenly language. Now the manager, along with the other employees, were running to the front to see what all the commotion was about. The manager said, "Do we need to call 911?" I said, "No she's fine, she's just praying." To tell you the truth, I didn't know what to say. This had never happened to me in this magnitude before. It wasn't your usual prayer line at church, this was in a public arena with no catchers for those who are slain in the Spirit. This young woman was being saturated with His presence. What an awesome experience, not just for her, but for me as well! You never know what might happen, that's why we've just got to stay ready, and I mean for anything.

On my way home, all I could do was laugh, and I believe God was laughing with me. I must say that there's no feeling in this world compared to the fulfillment you'll experience when you've had the privilege of leading someone to Him.

If You Can't Get To Them

In the month of January, 2011, I went to Little Rock, Arkansas, to spend a week with a friend who just had surgery. Instead of me taking care of her at home, she arranged for us to stay at an exclusive hotel near the hospital. After two days of being there, I had the urge to impart into someone's life, but I didn't want to leave my friend for any length of time. That afternoon, a housekeeper knocked on our door, and after she gave us our linens, I had the opportunity to witness to her and lead her to the Lord. Later that day, she brought another maid to our suite for prayer. Once again, another soul received salvation. The next day, a knock came on our door. "Housekeeping!" But she wasn't there just to clean our room. She said, "My friend sent me here," so I invited her in. Well, she left differently than when she came. Though I didn't expound on each individual's experience, I can tell you that their heartfelt tears conveyed a message of sincerity as they made earnest decisions for

Christ. I guess you could say that our hotel living room became a sanctuary, a place of consecration. You see, if you can't get to them, He'll bring them to you.

Here are just a few goals that I have set for myself, and the Lord may give you more creative ideas.

Each day that you witness to someone, write their name down in your date book, and where you were at the time; whether it's in a supermarket, department store, at work, your church, by phone, email, or even texting. Not only does this set a goal for you to witness, but you have those names to pray over when you feel the leading. You'll be amazed and encouraged at the end of one year on how many people you were able to witness to.

Remember to always give them scriptures on the back of your business or ministry card before you leave them. You see, they may forget what you say, but His Words will go with them and last forever.

I've had many people tell me that they still have the card I'd given them years prior. They would get it out and read the scriptures over and over, especially when they were going through challenging circumstances.

The Card

I witnessed to one lady named Lynn in a department store, and then I gave her my card along with scriptures on the back. After reading those verses, she rededicated her life to the Lord. Four years later, one summer evening, Lynn decided to treat her mother to dinner. Ironically, they were seated at a table beside my brother, Tim. He's a likeable pastor that never meets a stranger. Well, it didn't take long for him to strike up a conversation with them.

Lynn and her mother were thinking, "Who is this guy?" After some chit-chat and laughter, he began to encourage her in the Lord. She looked at him and said, "You remind me of someone." Then she proceeded to tell him about meeting a lady a few years ago that led her back to the Lord. She said, "Since that time, I've wanted to reconnect with her and tell her what God has done in my life." Tim said, "What did she look like?" As she began to describe me, he said, "That sounds like my sister." She said, "No way." Lynn said, "Just a minute, I'll be right back." She went out to her car to get her planner book, and as soon as she opened it, she saw my card protruding up. She hurried back into the restaurant to show him. When she got to Tim's table she said, "Is this your sister?" He smiled and said, "It sure is." She couldn't believe it, but the story doesn't end here. One year had past and she became established in a church close to their home. Little did she know, that this church supported our ministry faithfully. We had even taken many of their members on mission trips.

On one particular Sunday, the church announced a large sale that would be held at our ministry facility. She looked at her mother and said, "Mom, we ought to go and support missions." Well, when she arrived at the Storehouse, she noticed the logo on our sign and with a puzzled look, she said, "That logo looks so familiar to me." Then she pulled out the card again. Obviously, the logo on the card matched the sign, so as soon as she walked in, she showed Rick the card and said, "Hi, do you know Debbie McNeely?" He said, "Yes, that's my wife." I had just left to get something from the house and as soon as I walked in the phone rang. It was Rick. He said, "There's some lady here wanting to see you." It had been five years since I had first witnessed to her. We hugged, exchanged words, then the Lord gave me another scripture for her concerning her ministry. In addition, her mother, Dorothy, was healed of a heart condition.

I had no idea that she previously had a heart attack which caused extensive damage. She spent many days in ICU before they released her. Dorothy's prognosis was fatal with a death sentence of only three months to live. Lynn valued each day with her mother, in so much that she took her with her just about everywhere she went. After I had ministered with Lynn, the Lord urged me to give Dorothy two scriptures on healing. They read:

"I will restore health to you and heal you of your wounds, says the Lord."   **-Jeremiah 30:17**

Fear not, for I am with you; be not dismayed, for I am your God. I will strengthen you, yes, I will help you, I will uphold you with My righteous right hand.   **-Isaiah 41:10**

I didn't even know she was sick, but God sure did. While the Word was being spoken over her, strength went all through her body. Tears of joy began to flow down her face as she felt His healing virtue. A few days later, she went to the doctor for an examination. As soon as he saw her he stated, "You shouldn't be alive!" Then he stared at her and shook his head. He proceeded, "I had nothing to do with this, it had to be a higher power." This was a documented miracle. To God be all the glory! That's been eight years ago, and she's still going strong. Dorothy is seventy-eight years old. She drives, takes care of her granddaughter, and works alongside of Lynn in women's ministry. Her healing is all in accordance with His Word. Remember:

He sent His word and healed them, and delivered them from their destructions.   **-Psalm 107:20**

There's power in God's Word! The Bible is nothing short of extraordinary! Archaeology continues to verify its history and confirm its validity, and after their findings they end up supporting scripture.

Closing Statements

We don't have the right to remain silent, we've been subpoenaed by His blood to take the Witness Stand, and testify for those who are standing trial. The fact is, we were all guilty, until Calvary proved us innocent, and unless we present the evidence of the cross, the convicted will remain guilty and be sentenced to Hell. Our testimony can make a difference for the falsely accused and the ones who are condemned to die. We must

Deliver those drawn toward death, and hold back those stumbling to the slaughter. **-Proverbs 24:11**

and make them aware of His love and unmerited favor. He's already paid the price, and has freed us from the law of sin and death;

Therefore if the Son makes you free, you shall be free indeed. **-John 8:36**

We have received this breaking news, The Good News, (which is the very definition of the Gospel) so we must broadcast it both far and near.

In conclusion, people are at ease when we are at ease with ourselves. They know when our smiles are real and if we genuinely care. It's not our eloquent words or our religious intellect that wins someone for Christ, it's simply making ourselves available and allowing Him to love through us. Listen to the Lord's last appeal:

But when He saw the multitudes, He was moved with compassion for them, because they were weary and scattered, like sheep having no shepherd. Then He said to His disciples, "The harvest truly is plentiful, but the laborers are few. Therefore pray the Lord of the harvest to send out laborers into His harvest." -**Matthew 9:36-38**

Jesus' heart was moved with compassion when He saw the multitudes scattered like sheep with no shepherd. His request to gather them was earnest, and now He's calling us to take the stand and be His witness.

I rest my case!